Selections from the

World's Devotional Classics

Volume II

Augustine to Suso

Augustine of Hippo

Selections
from the
World's
Devotional
Classics

EDITED BY
Robert Scott and George W. Gilmore
Editors of The Homiletic Review

IN TEN VOLUMES

Volume II
Augustine to Suso

FUNK & WAGNALLS COMPANY
NEW YORK AND LONDON

Contents Volume Two

Selections

PAGE

From The Meditations, The Manual, and The
    Confessions of St. Augustine (*Frontis-
    piece*) 1
From The Sermons of Leo the Great, Bishop
    of Rome 85
From The Proslogium of St. Anselm 103
From The Sermon on the Song of Solomon,
    and The Devout Meditations of Saint
    Bernard of Clairvaux (*Illustration*) .. 127
The Canticle of the Sun, by Saint Francis of
    Assisi (*Illustration*) 179
From The Works of Jan van Ruysbroeck .. 183
From The Little Book of Eternal Wisdom,
    and The Maxims, by Heinrich Suso .. 191

Prayers

A Prayer of Charles How 125
A Prayer of Ludovicus Palamo 126
A Prayer of James Russell Miller 177
An Ancient Collect 182
A Prayer of Thomas Treadwell Stone 216

vii

SELECTIONS FROM

The Meditations, The Manual

AND

The Confessions

OF

ST. AUGUSTINE

AUGUSTINE

Bishop of Hippo, Father of the Church, preacher, and controversialist; born at Thagaste in proconsular Numidia, November 13, 354; died at Hippo Regius, August 28, 430. He was educated at Madaura and Carthage, and during his early life his mother, Monnica, was his closest instructor. Carthage, the second city of the empire, was rank as Rome in its sensual corruptions, and Augustine succumbed to its seductions. Later he accepted the doctrines of the Manichæans. In his native town he lectured for a short time on "grammar," *i.e.*, literature, then returned to Carthage. In 383 he went to Rome; next he taught rhetoric in Milan, where the eloquent and devout Ambrose was bishop. In his thirty-first year he was strongly attracted to Neoplatonism. One day he seemed to hear a voice saying *Tolle, Lege,* "Take up and read." He turned to the Bible and read from Romans 13:14, "Put ye on the Lord Jesus Christ, and make not provision for the flesh, to fulfil the lusts thereof." From this dated his conversion to Christianity, and on April 25, 387, he was baptized by Ambrose. In 391 he was ordained priest by Valerius, bishop of Hippo in Numidia, to whom he became coadjutor, and succeeded as bishop in 396. Into the Donatist and Pelagian controversies he entered keenly as a defender of the orthodox faith. Among his writings may be mentioned: "The Confessions" (397); the "Epistles" (270 in the Benedictine edition), variously dated between 386 and 429; "On Free-Will" (388-395); "On Christian Doctrine" (397); "On Baptism: Against the Donatists" (400); "On the Trinity" (400-416); "On Nature and Grace" (415); "The City of God" (426); and "Homilies" upon several books of the Bible.

The Meditations of St. Augustine

A Prayer for Reformation of Life

Inspire my soul, O Lord my God, with a holy desire of thee, my chief, my only good, that I may so earnestly desire as diligently to seek thee, so successfully seek as to be happy in finding thee; make me so sensible of that happiness in finding as most passionately to love thee; so effectually to express that love as to make some amends for my past wickedness, by hating and forsaking my former evil courses and entering upon a conversation exemplarily pious for the time to come.

Give me, dear God, hearty repentance, an humble and contrite spirit; make my eyes a fountain of tears, and my hands liberal dispensers of alms and unwearied instruments of good works. Thou art my King; reign absolute in my heart, subdue and expel thence all rebellious passions; quench all the impure burnings of fleshly lusts, and kindle in it the bright fire of thy love.

Thou art my Redeemer, beat down and drive out the spirit of pride, and impart to me, in much mercy, the treasure of thy own unexampled humility, and wonderful condescension.

Thou art my Savior, take from me the rage of anger; and arm me, I beseech thee, with the shield of patience.

Thou art my Creator, root out from me all that rancor and malice whereby my nature is corrupted; and implant in me all that sweetness and gentleness of temper, which may render me a man made in thy own image and after the likeness of thy own divine goodness.

Thou art my most merciful and indulgent Father, O grant thy own child those best of gifts; a firm and right faith, a stedfast and well-grounded hope, and a never-failing charity.

O my Director and Governor, turn away from me, I beseech thee, vanity and filthiness of mind, a wandering heart, a scurrilous tongue, a proud look, a gluttonous belly; preserve me from the venom of slander and detraction, from the itch of curiosity, from the thirst of covetousness, ambition and vainglory; from the deceits of hypocrisy, the secret poison of flattery; from contempt of the poor, and oppression of the helpless; from the canker of envy, the fever of avarice, and the pestilential disease of blasphemy and profaneness.

Prune away my superfluity of naughtiness, and purge me from all manner of injustice, rashness, and obstinacy; from impatience, blindness of heart, and cruelty of disposition.

Incline me to obey that which is good, and to comply with wholesome advice; enable me to bridle my tongue and to contain my hands from wrong and robbery. Suffer me not to insult the poor, to defame the innocent, to despise my inferiors, to treat my servants with severity and scorn, to fail in due affection toward my friends and relations or in kindness and compassion toward my neighbors and acquaintances.

O my God, thou Fountain of mercy, I beg thee, for the sake of the Son of thy love, dispose me to the love and practise of kindness and mercy; that I may have a tender fellow-feeling of my brethren's afflictions, and apply myself cheerfully to rectify their mistakes, to relieve their miseries, to supply their wants, to comfort their sorrows; to assist the opprest, to right the injured, to sustain the needy, to cherish the dejected, to release them that are indebted to me, to pardon them that have offended me, to love them that hate me, to render good for evil, to despise none, but pay all due respect to every man. Give me grace to imitate those that live well, to avoid and beware of them that do ill; to follow all manner of virtue, and utterly abandon and

detect all sort of vice: make me patient in
adversity, and moderate in prosperity. "Set
a watch before my mouth, and keep the door
of my lips"; wean my affections from things
below, and let them be eager and fixt upon
heaven and heavenly things.

A Prayer To the Holy Ghost

And now, O Holy Spirit, Love of God, who
proceedest from the Almighty Father and his
most blessed Son, powerful Advocate, and
sweetest Comforter, infuse thy grace, and
descend plentifully into my heart; enlighten
the dark corners of this neglected dwelling,
and scatter there thy cheerful beams; dwell
in that soul which longs to be thy temple;
water that barren soil, overrun with weeds
and briars and lost for want of cultivating,
and make it fruitful with thy dew from heav-
en. Heal the lurking distempers of my inward man; strike me through with the dart
of thy love, and kindle holy fires in my breast,
such as may flame out in a bright and devout
zeal, actuate and enliven the heavy mass,
burn up all the dross of sensual affections,
and diffusing themselves through every part,
possess, and purify, and warm my whole
spirit and soul and body.

Make me to drink of the spiritual pleasures

6

as out of a river; and let their heavenly sweetness so correct my palate as to leave no desire, no relish, for the gross unhealthful fulsomeness of the worldly delights. "Judge me, O Lord, and defend my cause against the ungodly people. Teach me to do that thing that pleaseth thee, for thou art my God." I believe, that in whomsoever thou dwellest, the Father and the Son do likewise come and inhabit that breast. And oh! happy is that breast, which is honored with so glorious, so divine a guest, in whose company the Father and the Son always come and take up their abode! O that it may please thee to come to me, thou kindest Comforter of mourning souls, thou mighty Defense in distresses, and ready Help in time of need. O come, thou Purger of all inward pollutions, and Healer of spiritual wounds and diseases. Come, thou Strength of the feeble, and Raiser of them that fall. Come, thou Putter down of the proud, and Teacher of the meek and humble. Come, thou Father of the fatherless, and just Avenger of desolate widows. Come, come, thou Hope of the poor, and Refreshment of them that languish and faint. Come, thou Star and Guide of them that fail in this tempestuous sea of the world; thou only Haven of the tossed and shipwrecked. Come, thou Glory and Crown of the living, and only Safeguard of the dying. Come, Holy Spirit, in much mercy, come, make me fit to receive thee, and condescend to my infirmities, that my meanness may not be disdained by thy greatness, nor my weakness by thy strength: all which I beg for the sake of Jesus Christ my only Savior, who in the unity of thee, O Holy Spirit, liveth and reigneth with the Father, one God, World without end. AMEN.

The Souls of the Righteous Are the House of God

This house of thine, my God, is not built of earthly, nor of any such heavenly, but corporeal matter, as the orbs above are formed of; but is spiritual and eternal, without flaw or decay. For thou hast set it fast for ever and ever, and founded it upon a decree which shall not be broken. Thou hast given it a duration equal to thy own, and end it shall have none, tho it had a beginning. For wisdom was created in the beginning. Not that essential Wisdom coeternal with the Father, by whom all things were made, but that which is created by spiritual substance, the rational and intellectual mind, which is light by contemplation of light, and in a qualified sense styled wisdom, tho it be finite and created.

But as there is a mighty difference between original light and that which is derived from and caused by the reflection of it; so is there between thee the perfect uncreated wisdom and that which is thy creature and thy image. Thus also we distinguish between the righteousness which justifies (the righteousness of God) and that which is attributed to the persons justified by it: in which last sense, the apostle says we are made the righteousness of God, in thee his Son, our Lord

The ground of which distinction lies in this, that the first of all these creatures was wisdom; that rational power of which thy city consists, which is above; and free, the chaste mother of us all, for ever in the heavens, even in that heaven of heavens which continually praises God, and is to him the heaven of heavens indeed. And tho we can assign no point of time antecedent to this noble workmanship of thine, which had a being before time itself was: yet thou the eternal Creator art before it, and from thee it derives its eternity and its beginning. It is therefore of thee in such a manner as to be a substance distinct from thee: it is qualified to behold thy face always, and never to be deprived of that blessed vision. In this respect it undergoes no change, and yet it is liable to change; for this light may grow dim and cold, if not

fed and kept bright by the fire of fervent
love, which when well cherished, conveys into
it a heat and luster clearer and warmer than
the noonday sun.

By this most holy love it is so closely
united to thee, the true, the eternal God, that
tho it be not of the same eternity from the
beginning, yet no length of future time, no
change of fortune or affairs, shall ever dis-
solve or loosen it; but it shall rest and be
employed for ever in the ravishing contemplation of thy divine excellencies. For thou,
O God, art bountiful to all that love thee;
and wilt reveal thyself to such as seek thee,
in measures large as their capacities admit, or
at least as their necessities require. This
keeps thy servants steady to thee and to themselves. This preserves the soul in the same
happy state, while its eyes are ever intent,
its affections ever fixt upon thee; while it
beholds and loves and delights in that God
who is true Light, and pure Love. O blessed
noble Creature the first and best of all the
works of God! but then most blest, when
dwelling upon thy Master's blessed perfections; then happy beyond all expression,
when entertaining that divine inhabitant, and
illustrated with the enlivening beams of that
glorious spring of light from on high!

What can I suppose deserves that magnifi-

cent name, the heaven of heavens? What can
be esteemed the highest and most beloved
habitation of God, rather than this spiritual
house; the purity and zeal of a mind at unity
in itself, always transported with the pleasure of beholding the divine glory; always
enamored with God without admitting any
rival and partner in its love. This is the
rock on which blessed spirits are built; these
the heavenly satisfactions in heavenly places;
this the foretaste of future joys and the
assurance of every wayfaring soul, that tho
it sojourn at present in a strange land and
at a great distance from thee, yet if it thirst
and pant after thee, if its godly tears are
its meat day and night, if the dwelling thus
above hereafter all the days of its life be its
constant wish and endeavor, its longing shall
one day be satisfied with the pleasures of thy
house, and all its pious mournings turned
into joy. From this bliss then and duration
of their own let our souls raise themselves
to form such ideas of thine as their present
condition can receive. For what notions
must we have of this blessedness, and how
vast is thy eternity, when even this created
house of thine, when keeping at home with
thee, tho it partake not of the same unbounded
eternity, yet by its union with its glorious
Maker and Inhabitant, stands proof against

all chance of time; and, persevering by thy gracious influences, is firm, notwithstanding the possibility of change which it is subject to: secured by thy presence, and by its own constant affection, and those liberal communications of thy grace which it drinks in and feasts upon continually: it looks at nothing beyond thee, as a future addition to its happiness; it is afflicted with no troublesome remembrances of anything past which should embitter or lessen the present, but is entirely blest with the enjoyment of that God who hath in mercy made it like himself, and knit it to himself with the strongest cement of inviolable love, and such a fulness of satisfaction as neither suffers nor desires a change.

A Prayer for Succor in Trouble and Danger

Blessed are all thy saints, my God and King, who have traveled over the tempestuous sea of mortality, and have at last made the desired port of peace and felicity; fearless of future hazards, and full of perpetual joy. This sea, thou, my Savior, didst condescend to try and be tossed upon. O cast a gracious eye upon us who are still in our dangerous voyage. Thou art possest of never-fading glory, but do not in the midst of thy own happiness forget those who are beset with vast variety of miseries. Thou hast chosen us to thyself, and what we are or hope to be is all thy gift; thou hast promised to make us immortal with and by thyself, and to bestow upon us the everlasting felicity of thy presence; O remember and succor us in our distress, and think on them who lie exposed to the rough storms of troubles and temptations.

Thou art the beautiful Gate of heaven, the Door at which the sheep must enter; but we alas! lie groveling here below, and our soul cleaveth to the dust. Stretch forth thy hand, and raise us up; strengthen our weakness, that we may do valiantly in this spiritual war, who of ourselves are not able to stand against the mighty force that comes against us. Help us against our enemies' power; help us against our own negligence and cowardice, and defend us from the treachery of our own unfaithful hearts. We are exceedingly frail, exceeding weak and despicable slaves to intemperance and lust, and indisposed to every virtuous and gallant undertaking. And yet, helpless wretches as we are, when lifted under thy banner and borne up by thy cross, we are buoyed up in faith, and commit ourselves boldly to this great and wide sea, wherein "are things creeping innumerable, both small

"and great beasts, where is that leviathan,"
that serpent ready to devour; wherein are
rocks and quicksands and other dangers with
out number, on which the careless and the
unbelieving run their vessels and suffer ship-
wreck daily.

Intercede for me therefore, most gracious
Savior, that, by thy powerful mediation and
all-sufficient merits, I may be able to bring
this vessel and its lading safe to shore; and
be conducted to the haven where every pious
soul would be, the haven of peace and salvation, of uninterrupted rest, and never-ending
joy.

An Act of Devotion and Love of God

O blessed Jesus, my Sacrifice and Ransom,
the Delight and Desire of my soul, God of
God! mercifully assist the prayers of thy
humble servant. On thee I call, to thee I
cry with a loud voice and from the very bottom of my heart. Thy presence I invite into
my soul, O enter there and fit it up for thyself, that it may not offend thee "by spot or
wrinkle or any such thing, but be holy and
without blemish." For surely a clean dwelling only can be acceptable to the purity of so
divine an Inhabitant. Do thou therefore
sanctify me, a vessel made by thy own hand,

and make me fit for thy own use: purge out all the remains of wickedness; fill me with thy grace, and keep me ever in that fulness that I may be built up a holy temple, an habitation such as my God will not disdain here and for ever. O sweetest, kindest, dearest, most powerful, most precious, loveliest and most beautiful Savior! more delicious than honey, whiter than snow, of more value than gold and precious stones, and dearer to me than all the riches, and honors, and pleasures this world can afford!

But what does all I have said amount to, my God, my only Hope, my unspeakable Mercy? What have I said, my sweet Repose, my sure Refuge, in all this? Alas! I say as much as I can, tho in no degree what I ought, upon so glorious a subject. O that I were capable of expressing thy excellencies in as perfect and becoming a manner as the melodious choirs of angels do in their perpetual consorts of praise! How gladly would I then spend all my breath, and even warble out my soul in songs of thanksgiving? With what ardent, what indefatigable devotion would I proclaim thy glories in the midst of thy congregations! But if I can not do so much as becomes me, is that a reason why I should do nothing? No, I will exert my utmost powers, and speak my best, tho I can

never speak enough: for wo to them that are
silent on this occasion; since them who are
willing thou renderest able, making even the
dumb to speak; and out of the mouths of
very babes and sucklings perfecting praise.
Wo then to them who do not employ their
tongues to thy honor, since even the greatest
masters of eloquence, who use them most and
best, yet in effect are dumb, and say nothing
to purpose, when they do not employ their
tongues to thy honor.

Who can set forth thy greatness as it deserves, O inexpressible Power and Wisdom
of the Father! But, in regard no words are
to be found sufficient to declare the omnipotent and omnipresent Word, I will at least
contrive the best I can, and go the greatest
length mortality is qualified for, till thou
shalt receive me to thy own self, and enable
me to express my praises in terms suitable
to thy dignity and my duty. In the meanwhile it is my earnest request that thou
wouldst measure my present feeble essays, not
by what I say, but what I desire to say. For
it is the most vehement wish and longing of
my soul to give such praises as I know are
becoming so great a Majesty to receive, and
a due homage for a creature to give. And
thou, my God, who knowest the secrets of all
hearts and art conscious of every motion of

my soul, canst bear me witness that heaven
and earth and all that therein is are of small
consideration with me in comparison with
thee. Whatever else may challenge a place
in my affection ceases to be of any regard
at all, and ought indeed to be hated when
put in the balance with my God. This is
the real sense of my soul, with such unrivaled,
such a fervent passion I love my God; and
yet am sensible withal, that this is less than
thy due, and therefore desire above all things
to love thee still more and more.

O grant that I may daily grow and continue for ever stedfast in thy love, that I
may pay thee all the affection I wish I could,
all I owe and should pay; that thou mayest
be my only aim and end, the only object of
my thoughts. Let my days be spent in medi-
tating upon thee incessantly; and my dreams
present no other idea to my imagination: let
my spirit confer with thee upon my bed, and
remember thee alone when waking in the night
season. Let the light of thy countenance
shine through every corner of my heart, that
under thy government and conduct I may
proceed strength to strength, till at length
I see the God of Gods in Zion; and whom I
now can only take an imperfect glimpse of
through a dark and broken glass, may then
behold face to face and know even as I am

known. And since this is a blessing promised in a peculiar manner to the pure in heart, I entreat thee, by all that goodness and compassion which hath delivered us from death eternal, let thy most powerful holy union soften this tough, hard, rocky heart of mine, and render it susceptible of tender and good impressions, that the fire of compunction and holy zeal may be cherished there continually, and render it a daily living sacrifice unto thee.

Grant me the grace of an humble and contrite spirit, that I may come into thy presence washed clean with tears of godly sorrow. And let my affections be so inseparably united to thee that I may have no carnal desires left, but be utterly cold and dead to this world. Let me not so much as remember transitory things for the vehemence of that fear and love I bear to God; that these momentary trifles may no longer be matter of grief or joy or concern to me, nor any flattering prosperity have power to bias or corrupt my heart, nor any terror of adversity to shake my constancy. And because the love of thee is strong as death itself, let this, I beseech thee, entirely possess and swallow up my soul; let that sweet and holy fire consume all the dross of worldly affections, that I may cleave to thee alone, and make it my constant meat and drink to do thy will, and know no refreshments but such as flow from the delightful remembrances of thee.

Send down, O Lord, send down into my heart thy precious odors, that I may be ravished with the fragrance of my heavenly spouse. Let the delightful relish of thy sweetness excite in me holy and eager desires, and be in me a well of living water springing up to everlasting life. Thy greatness, O my God, is unmeasurable, and therefore the love of thee ought to be so too; for sure no bounds ought to determine the gratitude and praise of those whom thou hast vouchsafed to redeem with thy own most precious blood. O tender Lover of souls! O merciful Lord! O righteous Judge, to whom thy Father hath committed all judgment! Thou seest and hast declared how fit it is that the children of this world should not in their generation be wiser than the children of light; that the sons of night and darkness ought to be our pattern; and that it is just a matter of reproach to us, if they shall love and pursue the perishing riches and fleeting pleasures and advantages with a more intense desire and more unwearied endeavors than thy own servants seek and love the source and sum of their true happiness: even thee their God, who made them when they were not, and re-

deemed them when otherwise it were better
for them not to have been at all.

And if one man love another man so fervently, if a spouse be so fond of her beloved
as not, without the utmost impatience and
even inconsolable grief, to bear the absence
of a friend so dear—what affection, what zeal,
what ardent desire of constant union, ought
that soul to express whom thou hast betrothed
and married to thyself by faithfulness and
mercies manifold? How ought we to be conversing with and enjoying the great God, the
most amiable husband, who hath loved us and
saved us after so astonishing a manner, and
for our sakes done so many, so great, so kind,
so wonderful things! For tho the objects
here below have indeed some delights peculiar to themselves, which attract our hearts
and kindle affections and desires proportioned
to them; yet do not they affect us after the
same manner as thou our God and the blessed
objects above do. The righteous man rejoices
in thee, because the love of thee is a calm and
sweet resentment. For every breast thus disposed is filled with an equal, secure, and
serene pleasure. But the love of the world
and the flesh is ruffled with anxious fears and
violent emotions: it utterly destroys the peace
of the soul where it takes possession, and distracts them with cares and suspicions, with

jealousy and passions, and a thousand uneasy apprehensions.

Most justly, therefore, art thou the Joy and Delight of good men, because thou art the only Haven where they are at rest; and with thee alone is that life which brings quietness and assurance, settled and sincere pleasure. He that enters into thee enters into the joy of his Lord, where fears of future evils have no place. Fixt in this most happy station, and secure from change or danger, he can speak comfort to his soul in these words of the psalmist, "this shall be my rest for ever; here I dwell, for I have a delight therein." And again, "The Lord is my Shepherd, therefore can I lack nothing: he shall make me to lie down in green pastures, and send me forth beside the still waters."

O that it might please my sweetest, dearest Jesus to fill my heart with such a love of him as never can be quenched; to be ever present in mind, that I may be all over love and burn with perpetual desires of his company and enjoyment. Let this desire exalt my heart, and enable it to throw off that troublesome load of sensual and worldly affections which now obstruct and press me down, and do but add to my miseries instead of gratifying my inclinations. And, "having laid aside this weight," help me to "run cheerfully and apace" after the odor of thy ointments, still keeping on my course without incumbrance or diversion, till by thy gracious guidance I at last shall be received to thy own self, there to be feasted for ever with the pleasures of thy beauteous presence.

For two so different passions, a good and an evil, a sweet and a bitter, can not dwell together in the same breast. And therefore, if a man love any thing besides thee, the love of God is not in him. O Love of exquisite pleasure, and exquisite Pleasure of love! Love, all Delight without allay of torment; Love, chaste and perfect, whose bright flame never can be extinct, but burns pure and cheerful to all eternity; my God, my Jesus, who art Love and Pleasure in the abstract, inflame my every part with this holy fire, pour thy transporting joys, thy inexpressible comforts and sweet raptures, abundantly into my soul; kindle there desires chaste and holy, peaceful and calm, pleasant and secure, that thus overflowing with delight and inflamed with desire, I may love thee, my God, with all my heart, and soul, and strength: that thou mayest be always in my mind, and mouth, and sight, at all times and in all places; and so refresh me that no room may be left for any other, which are indeed no better than unfaithful and adulterous passions.

Hear me, my God; hear, thou Light of my eyes, hear what I ask, and grant my petitions; and that thou mayest hear me effectually, do thou inspire and direct my petitions. O merciful and gracious Lord! let not my manifold offenses stop thy ears against my prayers, nor shut out thy mercy from me: but let thy servant obtain his requests, tho not for any merit of his own, yet for the sake of his merits and intercession in whom alone he trusts, and by him only presumes to ask any thing: even the blessed Jesus, the Son of thy love, the one powerful Mediator between God and man; who with thee and thy blessed Spirit liveth and reigneth for ever. AMEN.

A Prayer in Time of Affliction

Look down, O Lord, with pity and compassion upon a most miserable sinner, doing the things he ought not, and enduring the things which he hath most justly deserved, every day multiplying his offenses, and smarting daily under thy correcting rod for them. When I reflect upon my many and great provocations, I can not but confess my sufferings light and gentle in comparison, and own they do by no means bear proportion to what I have incurred and might expect. Righteous art thou, O Lord, and just are thy judgments. Yea, just and faithful is my God, and there is no iniquity in him. Thou sendest affliction, but thou sendest it upon creatures and upon sinners, and canst not therefore be charged with injustice or cruelty. For what is the utmost we groan under? How does this declare thy power, in comparison with that almighty instance of it which commanded us into being when we were not? How does this deserve the imputation of rigor, when set against that infinite mercy which in wonderful pity redeemed and restored us to happiness and life, when sin had reduced us to a condition so lost and desperate that even our being had become a curse to us?

I am abundantly convinced that the events of this life are not left to the rash, uncertain hits of blind chance, but under the steady governance and wise disposal of thy good providence. I know thou lovest and takest care of all thy creatures, but more especially thy faithful servants, who repose all their hope and confidence in thy mercy, and in this confidence do cheerfully commit themselves and all their affairs to thee. In this persuasion I most humbly pray thee that thou wouldst deal with me not according to my sins, which have made me obnoxious to thy angry justice, but after thy own great mercy, which far exceeds not only mine, but the whole world's offenses. And may it please thee, when thou thinkest fit to scourge my outward man, to strengthen my inward with the grace of constancy and unwearied patience; that even in the bitterest anguish of my soul thy goodness may still be acknowledged most thankfully, and thy praise at no time depart out of my mouth. Pity me, O Lord, and help me, according to what thou seest necessary for me both in body and soul. Thou knowest all things, and canst do all things, and livest for ever, and therefore wilt, I hope, consider my needs and my infirmities, and extend mercy and relief in thy own time and thy own way, which is always sure to be best and most expedient for us.

Love, the Way That Leadeth to Life

By what means we may avoid the torments of hell and attain the joys of heaven is an inquiry which deserves our most attentive application of thought; a science to be learned at the expense of our most watchful care and most solicitous concern. And in this study it is of great consequence to set out right; for all our most assiduous endeavors will be employed to very little purpose, if we be not first instructed what way it is that leads to everlasting bliss, and carries us out from all danger of everlasting misery. It will therefore behoove us very diligently to consider those words of the apostle in 1 Cor. 2:9, which, taken in their just latitude, do plainly teach us these two things: first, that the glories of the blest in a future state are greater than can be exprest; and then, secondly, what is the way by which we must arrive at this blessedness. "Eye," he says, "hath not seen, nor ear heard, neither hath it entered into the heart of man to conceive the things which God hath prepared for them that love him." Now when he tells us that these excellent things are prepared for them that love God, from thence the inference is natural and plain, that love is the condition enjoined in order to the obtaining them. But then the Scripture makes it no less evident that the love of God and the love of our neighbor are virtues inseparable from each other. For thus much is the importance of that passage in St. John, "He that loveth not his brother whom he hath seen, how can he love God whom he hath not seen?" And this commandment have we from him, that "he who loveth God loveth his brother also." In these two parts it seems that true charity consists, to which St. Paul hath given so glorious a character when he shuts up his discourse of the extraordinary gifts of the Spirit with those remarkable words: "And yet shew I unto you a more excellent way." Charity then is not only the way, but the best, nay, the only way, that leads to our heavenly country; for it is impossible for any man ever to come thither by any other way. But who is it that knows or walks in this way? Even he that loves God and his brother. It will concern us then to be perfectly well informed what are the proper expressions of our love to each, and the just measures of our affection to God and to our neighbor. And of this point it may suffice to say that we are bound in duty to love God more than ourselves, and to love our neighbor as ourselves. Now we love God more than ourselves, when upon all occasions we prefer his will before our own, and suffer no private interest or sensual inclination to come in competition with his commands and his honor. But it is very observable that, altho we are enjoined to love our neighbor as ourselves, yet we are nowhere enjoined to love him as much as we do ourselves; and therefore our duty in this respect is satisfied when we heartily wish and endeavor all that good to our neighbor which we ought to wish and endeavor the attainment of ourselves, especially the everlasting happiness of the soul; when we contribute to his obtaining it, and omit no instance whereby our help may be of any use to him in procuring any advantage, whether temporal or spiritual, so far as the present circumstances of affairs render our assistance seasonable, and our own condition puts it in our power to become serviceable to him. This explication agrees exactly with the equity of our Lord's rule, "Whatsoever ye would that men should do unto you, do ye even so to them." And it shews us likewise the necessity of that other left us by St. John, "Let us not love in word, neither in tongue, but in deed and in truth." But it may be asked once more, who those neighbors are whom we are bound to love after this manner? And to this the answer is very short, that the command is of unlimited extent, and comprehends all mankind; whether they be Christians, Jews, or infidels; whether they be acquaintances or strangers, whether they be friends or enemies.

Of the Love of God Toward Us

First then, it is necessary that every man should take a distinct view of himself, and when he is arrived at a due understanding of the honorable post God hath placed him in, that he be careful not to dishonor himself, nor injure his Maker, by settling his affections upon things that are below or unworthy of his character. For objects which, considered singly and separately, may appear beautiful and lovely, do yet deservedly sink in esteem when compared with others confessedly more excellent. It argues great folly to put things manifestly deformed and vile upon the level with such as are amiable and handsome; and is it a point of wisdom to raise those which have a noble and real excellence, and neither depending upon mere fancy nor of the meanest rank of beauties, to an equal degree with the highest and most eminently good? Consider then, my soul, what excellencies thou art endued with, and from hence take thy measures, what excellencies those are that deserve thy love. Now if, through negligence or long disuse of the most exalted objects, thy eyes are so far blinded that thou canst not entertain such lofty ideas of thy own condition as the case requires, yet thus far at least conquer thy own prejudices as to learn to make a just estimate of thyself by the judgment which another hath made of thee. And for this thou canst not want opportunity, because the matter is so plain as to give thee sufficient direction. Thou hast a Lord and Spouse, but how exquisitely beautiful as yet thou dost not perfectly know, because thou hast not seen his face. He sees

and knows thee thoroughly; for had he not
done so, he would not love thee. He hath
not thought fit hitherto to present himself to
thee, but he hath made thee many noble
presents, and given such pledges of his kindness as might at once be both assurances and
signs who it is that hath betrothed thee to
himself, and how exceeding tender that affection is, which moved him to this union.
Couldst thou behold his charms, there could
be no longer ground of doubt. For thou
wouldst be convinced, that one so fair, so
heavenly sweet, one of such matchless excellence, could not be smitten with thee, were
there not in thy form somewhat very grace-
ful, very uncommon, to recommend thee, and
engage his love. But in the meanwhile, how
dost thou behave thyself upon this occasion?
See him face to face thou canst not, because
he is absent; and is this a sufficient reason
for not paying him reverence, for insolently
and shamelessly affronting him, for slighting
that love which thou canst not but see, and
impudently prostituting thyself to the lust
of seducing strangers? O do not treat him
after this contemptuous manner! It thou
canst not as yet know all the charms of thy
lover, yet thou canst understand the valuable
instances of his love. These are already actually in thy possession; and, if considered

as they ought, will plainly shew thee what returns of love it becomes thee to make, and how extremely solicitous thou oughtest to be not to displease, not to despise, not to lose him or his favor. The pledge he hath given thee is most extraordinary—a noble gift suited to the majesty of the Giver. And, as it was below so great a person to bestow a thing of little value; so were it no less unbecoming so wise a person to throw away things of the highest value upon one in whom there was little or nothing valuable. Great therefore is the present he hath made, but greater still in his esteem is that which he loves in thee, and which induced him to give it.

But thou perhaps wilt ask, my soul, what this great gift is, which thy Spouse hath shewed himself so very bountiful in bestowing upon thee. Look round this universe, view every part of it, and tell me if thou canst there discover anything which does not some way or other do thee service. Is not this the end to which every creature seems to have been designed? And does not the whole course of nature plainly promote it? The gratifying of thy desires, the bringing in of thy profit, the supplying of thy wants, the furnishing of store for thy comforts and delights, the doing of all this in great abundance, and consulting not barely thy neces-

sities, but even thy ease and pleasure. This
is what the heavens, the earth, the air, the
sea, and all the inhabitants and products of
each of them are with a continual and most
efficient diligence employed about. The regu-
lar revolutions of time, the various seasons
of the year, the stated successions of night
and day, by which the world dies and re-
vives, grows old and young again; its fabric
ruined and repaired, its provisions consumed
and recruited; all is contrived so admirably
for thy purpose, that, as none of these vicissitudes are useless, so one can not conceive
how any of them could be spared without
some manifest, some insupportable inconve-
nience. This I suppose thee sensible of; but
art thou not sensible at the same time who
it is that framed and contrived this wonderful order, and disposed every part so ad-
vantageously that whatever discord appears
between each other, yet are all unanimous
in promoting the common design, and con-
spire to do thee service? How brutish is it
to feed upon the benefit, and remain ignorant
of thy benefactor? The gift is evident, and
is the giver a secret? Nay, thy own reason
will not allow thee an imagination so vain
that these advantages seem upon any account
thy due, or of thy own procuring, but loudly
tells thee thou owest them all to the liberality

of another. Now be that who it will to whose bounty thou art so largely indebted, it is plain he hath given us much; and no less plain that he, who gave so much, would not have done it, had he not loved much. So the greatness of his affection and the indispensable obligation to ours in return are both of them demonstrable from the quality of his gift. Now how extravagantly foolish is it not to desire the true love of one who hath it in his power to be so excellent a Friend? Not to do it of our own accord, and in regard to our interest, tho there were no antecedent obligation? But how impious, how perverse, how base, not to love him in return, who hath been so inexpressibly kind to us! If then thou lovest other things besides, do it with such limitations as are proper; maintain thy character, and remember theirs; love them as things below thee, as those that were made to do thee service, as tokens of thy Spouse's love, the gift of a Friend, the bounty of a Master; but be sure never to forget whose goodness all these blessings are owing to, and therefore be not fond of them for their own sake; but for his sake who bestowed them: nor let them divide thy affections with the Donor, for to take them into thy heart together with him is a wrong and great indignity, and therefore they must be loved for

him, but he by and for them, and infinitely
above them all.

God's Tender Care and Constant Presence With Us

Still I must repeat my grateful acknowledgment, that the blessings I have received
from thee are great beyond measure, and
many beyond number; of thee it shall be my
most delightful entertainment always to be
talking; and, Lord, I beseech thee, grant me
a mind truly thankful, that my mouth may
be ever full of thy praise, and my heart overflow with thy love, for thy infinite goodness
to me. Thou seest, my soul, what noble
pledges thou hast, and these pledges sufficiently declare the affection of that spouse
who gave them. Take care then to preserve
thy charity and fidelity entire. Let no impure desires, no adulterous lust, pollute or
divide thy affection; but keep thee only unto
him to the last moment of thy life. If thou
wert formerly an harlot, yet now thy virgin
innocence is restored. For such is the excellence of his wonderful love that it restores
purity to them that had lost it, and preserves
it unblemished to them who are careful to
retain it. Let then the greatness of his mercy
never slip out of thy mind, but consider how

tenderly he loved thee, who never was wanting to thee in any demonstration of his kindness which thy condition required. I can not but confess, when I reflect upon the constant presence and the abundance of his mercies toward me, that I am almost tempted to say that my salvation is his only business and care. For sure he could not be more tender of my safety, more ready to relieve all my distresses, to comfort all my sorrows, to supply all my wants, to guard me in all my dangers, could he be supposed to overlook the exigencies of all his other creatures, and confine his good providence to me alone. So watchful does he shew himself over all my affairs, so ever present to, nay, ever preventing (*i.e.*, anticipating) my earliest wishes. Wheresoever I go, he forsakes me not; wheresoever I am, he stands by me; whatsoever I do, he strengthens and succors me; he is a constant observer of all my behavior; and such is his goodness that whatever commendable attempts I make, he works together with me in them, and by the success which I attain gradually shews me that he condescends to work, not according to the efficacy of his own almighty power, but in proportion to my weak capacity. These instances make it indisputably clear that tho the imperfection of our present state will not allow us to see his face, yet we can not be so stupidly blind as not to be sensible of his presence—a presence which can no more be concealed than it can be avoided.

But while my thoughts are engaged upon this subject, I feel a new and unusual pleasure, that makes such strong, such delightful impressions as seem to transport and carry me out of myself. Methinks I am in an instant changed and become quite another creature, and joys come flowing in upon me more exquisite than I am able to express. My conscience is all over satisfaction; the anguish of my past sufferings is quite swallowed up, and not so much as a troublesome remembrance of them left behind. My mind is enlarged, my understanding clear and bright, my heart and its affections enlightened and purified, all my desires filled with pleasure, and my soul is perfect rapture and triumph. I am no longer here, methinks, but translated, I know not how nor whither, to some unknown region of bliss; I embrace, as it were, with a most ardent love, some dear object with which I am not yet perfectly acquainted: I hold him fast, and strive all I can never to part with him more; but still it is with a sort of delightful difficulty that I struggle not to let that break from me which of all things I wish to keep for ever in my arms. For in him my soul seems to have found the complement and end of all her desires. This thought creates that eager and inexpressible transport of joy; that she seeks nothing, covets nothing beyond it; but would esteem her happiness complete, could she continue always to be as now she is. What can this delicious object be that pours in such a torrent of rapturous and uncorrupted pleasure? Is it my Beloved? Undoubtedly it can be none but he. 'Tis thus the Lord vouchsafes to visit me. He comes in secret, not to be seen, not to be discerned by any of my senses. He comes to touch me, but not to shew me his face. He comes to put me in mind of him, but not to let me perfectly understand him. He comes to me to give me a taste of his sweetness, but not to give me his whole self; to gratify my desires, but not to bestow upon me the fulness of his excellencies. However, this is what my condition will admit, what I ought to receive with all the thanks and gladness possible: for it is an assured foretaste of heaven, an inviolable earnest and token of his marrying me to himself. And blessed, ever blessed be thy mercy, for these assurances, these comfortable antepasts of future happiness: thou, Lord, art good and gracious, and canst not worthily be praised for those supporting consolations whereby

thou, who hast promised that my soul shall
have a distinct view and full possession of
thee hereafter, doth convince her how sweet
that enjoyment, and how precious the promises of it are, by condescending to give her a
taste of thee here.

The Benefit of a Holy Hope

By being enabled to vanquish temptations,
I am put into a condition of escaping eternal
death; but it is yet a farther instance of
mercy that the Lord my God affords me such
grace as may qualify me for inheriting the
blessings of eternal life. And this I take
chiefly to consist in three things: the hatred
of past evil, the contempt of present good, and
the desire of that good which is to come;
which desire is also supported and inflamed
by another precious gift of God, the hope of
obtaining that future blessedness. Now there
are likewise three considerations which uphold and strengthen my heart in this hope,
and that so firmly that no want of desert on
my part, not even the lowest and most mor-
tifying thoughts of my vileness and unwor-
thiness nor the highest and most enlarged
notions of the excellence of that bliss in heav-
en can cast me down from this high tower
of hope. No, my soul is rooted and grounded

in it, past the power of being shaken with any melancholy misgivings. And the foundations that bear me up in all this firmness of mind are three. First, I consider the greatness of God's love, exprest in my adoption. Secondly, the truth of God, which hath promised this blessedness. And, thirdly, the power of God to make good whatever he hath promised, to the uttermost. Let then my foolish desponding heart raise scruples to confound me and object never so importunately: "Vain man, consider what thou art, and what thou fondly imaginest thou shalt one day be; what canst thou see in thyself, a creature so little, so polluted, to think that ever thou shouldst attain to a state of such purity, such excellent glory? Canst thou discern any proportion at all between a finite creature and infinite happiness? Or art thou able to discover any such extraordinary merit to ground thy hopes upon, as should incline God to exalt thee so much above what nature seems to have qualified thee for? These difficulties I am in no degree terrified by, but can with great assurance return this answer to them, and rest my soul upon it: "I know whom I have believed, and am verily persuaded," that God would never have adopted me for his own child, had he not loved me exceedingly; that he would never have promised

had he not resolved to perform; and that, if
these things could be supposed greater than
really they are, yet the putting me in actual
possession of them can not exceed his
power, because I am sure he can do whatsoever pleaseth him, both in heaven and earth.
And therefore I can never love God enough
for inspiring and comforting me with this
hope, and putting me into the way of attaining the bliss he hath encouraged me to expect
at his merciful hands. And great encourage-
ment I have from those earnests and antepasts of his future goodness, which he vouchsafes me even in this world. For such, I
reckon, are his following after and overtaking
me when I fled away from him; his controlling
and vanishing my fears, by the charms of
meekness and kindness, cherishing and frequently reviving my hopes, when I lay languishing in despair; his even constraining me
to better obedience by heaping on fresh benefits; notwithstanding my ingratitude for those
I had formerly received; his giving me a
better sense of things, and enabling me to
relish the sweetness of spiritual joys, when
my palate stood to none but such as were
impure and merely sensual; his bursting my
bonds asunder, and setting me at liberty
from the bondage of evil habits, which I had
not the power to break; and his receiving me

with so much tenderness, when by his help
I had weaned my affections from the world
and forsaken all to follow him. He would
not have done thus much for me already, had
he not intended to do more hereafter; and
therefore I will trust his word for this fulness
of bliss in reversion, and dare depend upon
the full accomplishment of it to his servant
(tho of myself most unworthy), since I have
such grounds of assurance from the many
precious pledges of an inviolable love ex-
hibited and paid me down in hand.

The Happiness of a Future State

Let us then raise our thoughts as high and
stretch them as wide as ever we can, that we
may try to represent to ourselves in some
measure the nature and perfection of that
joy of the saints, which no other is equal,
no other like unto. Now that chief good,
which we find called by the several titles of
life, light, blessedness, wisdom, eternity, and
the like, is but one most simple and supreme
good, perfect and self-sufficient, without which
no other thing can either be perfect or indeed be at all: this good, I say, is God the
Father, this the Word, or Son of God, this
again is that pure undivided love common to
Father and Son, both—the Holy Ghost,

I mean, who proceedeth from the Father and the Son. Now such as each of these persons is, considered apart by himself, such is the whole Trinity taken together; Father, Son, and Holy Ghost: for each of these singly is nothing else but the one most simple, constant Being which can neither be multiplied, nor diversified, nor changed. Here then is that one thing which is necessary: for that must certainly be a necessary good, in which all good is, nay, which itself is good, the one whole and sole good. If each of these things which we call good minister so much delight, how much must flow from the possession of him who comprehends them all, and is as much superior to them in excellence, as the Creator is above the creature? Let us not then lavish away our time and pains upon things that only flatter us with deceitful promises of happiness; but let us love this one good, for that alone can suffice for all our exigencies and fill all our largest desires. It is but lost labor to attempt a just description of the bliss reserved for us in our heavenly Father's kingdom; no words can express, no mind confined in flesh can expand itself sufficiently to conceive them. For when we have let loose our thoughts, still those joys are of a compass larger than they can fetch. Many and glorious things indeed have been spoken of this city of God, but yet the half of the truth hath not been told us. This is the only instance in which report can never exceed, and praises can never flatter; no knowledge can come up to it, no glory compare with it. The kingdom of God, in a word, is full of light and peace, charity and meekness, honor and glory, sweetness and love, joy and everlasting bliss, in short, of everything that is good, more and better than can be possibly exprest or conceived. But still this is no argument why I should not speak of it at all, or represent its excellencies as well as I can, because I can not do it so well as I would. We believe the majesty of God to be unspeakably glorious; but surely no man is so extravagant as to infer from thence that we ought never to speak of him, nay, it follows rather, that we should speak the most glorious things we are able, that they who hear us may believe him to be still far above all we can say of him. Much more, it is evident, may be comprehended by the understanding than a man can find proper words to utter; and yet the most profound and capacious mind can not comprehend or have any ideas of the kingdom of heaven in any degree suitable to its real excellence. And therefore the life to come is what we have represented to us by the following character, that it is eternal in duration, and a blessedness to all eternity, a state where there is the most profound security and tranquility, pleasure without passion, love without fear, love in perfection, day without night, activity and strength without possibility of decay, perfect unanimity, all the souls in it rapt with the contemplation of God, and past all apprehension of being ever deprived of his beatific presence: a city blest with the most glorious inhabitants, where all the saints and angels take up their perpetual residence; the splendor whereof consists in the shining graces of God's elect; where health abounds, and truth reigns for ever! where there is no deceiving, no being deceived; out of which none of the happy are ever expelled, into which none of the wretched are ever admitted.

This is that happy contemplative life which they who can reach up to, by the finishing of their virtues, shall for ever enjoy, and be like tLe spirits of just men made perfect, and shall reign with them for ever. What such have here anticipated by faith, they shall there have in sight; beholding with pure hearts the substance of their Creator; rejoicing with never-ceasing and exceeding great joy; united inseparably to God and to each other by the full fruition of the divine goodness and the charms of mutual love; then shall their once scattered bodies be restored and put on immortality and incorruption; and thus united, they shall be made free subjects of their heavenly country, and invested with all the privileges of the city of God. Then shall they reap the fruits of all their holy labors, those eternal recompenses the promises and distant expectation whereof sustained their spirits in the many long and painful conflicts here below. A general gladness there shall overflow, and these joys shall be so agreeable that they shall always be thankful to their bountiful Rewarder for the plenty he hath so nobly enriched them with, and yet that plenty shall abate no man's satisfaction in the abundance he enjoys. There every man's heart shall be open to every man, for every breast shall be so white and pure that the soul so cleansed shall find cause to thank God for washing away their stains in the blood of his Son, but not at all to be ashamed nor blushing for any of their old blemishes: and why should they not see into one another's hearts freely, who have no secrets in reserve, no separate interest to promote, no deceit to manage, no faults to conceal? For neither sins nor sinners are in heaven, and they who once were such, from the instant of their entering that place of purity, are out of all possibility ever to be so any more. None of the darkest secrets, none of the deepest mysteries, shall then continue such: the blessed shall be let into a distinct knowledge of them; and, which is infinitely better, they shall be ever viewing and admiring the adorable perfections of God himself.

This human nature shall then be advanced to its just and utmost perfection, incapable of being exalted or sunk lower any more. All the excellencies communicated to it, by being made after the likeness of its Maker, shall then be set at their highest pitch; and the corruption and defects introduced by sin utterly done away. Nay, we shall even rise above what was given us at our first creation, tho we had been so happy as to retain our primitive advantages. We shall understand and judge without error, remember without forgetfulness, think without wandering, love without dissimulation; we shall have sense without anything to offend it, ease without pain, life without death, power of acting without obstruction, fulness without nauseating, and such a perfection of every faculty that there shall be in us all imaginable soundness and vigor without any sort of disease or decay. Whatever maim our bodies may have suffered here, by sudden disasters, or wasting distempers, or mortified sores; whatever limbs have been lost by the biting of wild beasts, or the cruelty of men no less barbarous than they by war, or fire, or any other dismembering accident; nay, even the weakness and deformities of sickness and old age, shall all be repaired at the general resurrection; every defect supplied, every loss restored, and the body complete in all its parts; sound, and youthful, beautiful and gay, shall it then, together with the soul, be clothed with everlasting health and immortality. So happy shall all the saints be at that day; but tho all shall be happy, yet will not they all be equally so; their blisses then will hold proportion to their virtues now; and one star differs from another star in that glory, because the merciful King of glory rewards every man according to his works.

The Manual of St. Augustine

An Act of Love and Devotion

I love thee, O my God, and desire to love thee every day more fervently. For thou art beautiful and amiable above the sons of men, and deservest an affection equal to thy own adorable and incomprehensible excellencies. Equal to the marvelous instances of goodness, of which thy tender care for, and unspeakable condescensions in working

out, the eternal salvation of mankind hath
given such plentiful, such astonishing proofs.
O let that fire descend into my heart which
burns with a bright and holy flame, never
languishing, never to be quenched. May
every part of me feel the kindly heat, may
it expand itself, and burn up every other passion: that all the dross of vain and polluted
passions and desires being entirely consumed,
I may be turned all into love, and know no
other object of that love but thee alone, my
dearest, sweetest and most lovely Savior.

By that most holy, that most precious blood,
which thou wert content to shed upon the
cross for our redemption, grant me, I beseech thee, the grace of a truly contrite and
devout heart, at all times; but then especially
when I approach thy majesty in prayers and
praises and thankful commemorations of the
mysterious methods of man's redemption,
that most stupendous, most conspicuous and
everlasting monument of the divine mercy.
When I (unworthy, I confess, of so high a
privilege) prostrate myself before thy altar,
and assist in that heavenly sacrifice which
thou, my undefiled High-priest, hath instituted
for a memorial and pledge of thy love, and
for the daily repair of those breaches which
sin and frailty make upon our souls, by these
frequent and lively representations of that

death and passion, by virtue whereof alone we are or can be saved.

While I attend upon these holy mysteries, let my mind, I most humbly pray thee, be sensibly comforted and my faith confirmed with the joys of thy blessed presence. Let me find thee nigh at hand, and be affected as becomes one who justly values the honor and happiness of such a union with thee. Let my spiritual delights be ravishingly sweet, my love of thee exceeding strong and ardent, my inward hungerings after thee refreshed. For thou art the bread of life, every day eaten, yet still whole and never consumed: Lord, grant me evermore this nourishment: thou art the Light eternal, never eclipsed, never extinct: O shine in my heart, warm, enlighten and sanctify me, that I may be a chosen vessel for thy use, purged from all wicked filth, filled with all grace, and ever preserving that fulness. So shall I spiritually feed upon thy flesh, and feel my soul effectually sustained in the strength of this heavenly repast; so shall I be nourished unto life indeed, and living of thee, and by thee, at last be conducted to thee, and for ever rest in thee.

O Banquet of Love, heavenly sweet, let my bowels be refreshed by thee, my inward part overflow with the nectar of thy love, and my soul burst out with zealous expressions of thy praise continually. My God is love itself, sweeter than honey to my mouth, sustenance and joy; make me to live and grow in thee, and correct my vitiated palate, that I may truly relish thy heavenly delights and lose all taste, all appetite for any other. Thou art the soul of my life, the staff of my hope, the end and sum of all my desires. O do thou possess my whole heart, preside over every faculty, direct my understanding, exalt my affections and quench the thirst of my longing soul with those rivers of pleasures which flow at thy right hand for evermore. Let every fleshly and turbulent desire be awed into silence, and all imaginations of things in heaven, and air, and earth, flee from before thee. Let dreams and fancied revelations; let every word, and sign, and thought give way; and even the soul itself stand mute, go out of itself, and be employed in the contemplation of thee alone; for thou art my hope and my only trust: and tho the vileness of my own condition, and especially the infinite faults and frailties of my life, might reasonably shut me out from any hope that so great and holy a God should admit so polluted a wretch into communion with him, yet since the Word of God hath condescended to dwell in my flesh, and united his divine to our human nature, I can with confidence look up to that powerful Intercessor at thy right hand, and will not doubt but I shall one day be exalted to the same blessed place, where my flesh and blood does in my Jesus already sit triumphant, to whom be praise and glory, honor and adoration, and thanksgiving for ever. AMEN.

The Pleasure of Meditating Upon God

How sweet, O gracious Lord, who in wonderful kindness hast so loved, and saved, enlivened, and sanctified, and exalted us, how inexpressibly sweet are the thoughts and the remembrance of thee! The more I dwell on these reflections, the more I feel my soul exhilarated and transported with them. The excellencies of thy nature and merciful dispensations of thy providence I contemplate with the most abstracted simplicity of thought that my present state is capable of, and feel the delights resulting from them swell to a pitch as high as this distance of a sojourner in a strange land admits. More I covet earnestly, and daily aspire after, and can but covet and aspire after, during my confinement to a body of flesh and frailty. I am wounded with the darts of thy love, and burn with eager desire of seeing and being inseparably united to him whom my soul longeth to enjoy. I will therefore stand upon my guard, and take good heed to my ways; I will sing with the spirit, and I will sing with the understanding, and exert my utmost activity in setting forth the praises of him who hath made me his own by a double title; first by creating, and then by renewing and restoring my nature. My soul shall mount above the highest heavens, and in desire dwell with thee continually; that however my bodily presence detain me here below, yet in my inclinations and affections I may reside above, and so my heart be where thou art, its best and most desirable treasure.

But pity, I beseech thee, gracious Lord, the impotence and infirmities of thy servant, who, the more he contemplates thine infinite majesty and goodness, the more conscious he is of his disability to raise up to the dignity of that subject. My heart is too narrow, and thy unbounded excellencies, thy beauty, and power, and glory, and love exceed the largest comprehensions of any human mind. As the brightness of thy majesty is inconceivable, so are the bowels of that everlasting mercy by which thou adoptest them for thy own children, and receivedst them to be one with thyself, whom thou at first createdst out of nothing.

Consider, O my soul, the greatness of this love, and the noble privileges accruing to thee from it. For if thou hast just notions of these things, thou wilt be perfectly convinced that if the enduring daily pains and sickness, nay, if the torments of hell itself for a season, were made the condition of beholding Christ in his glory and being received into the number and society of the blessed above, no sufferings could be so exquisite that they ought not to be gladly entertained, none which would not find themselves abundantly recompensed by obtaining a portion in that transcendent felicity. What tho the devils then lay wait for us, and draw us into sharp trials of our virtue; what tho this body be macerated with fasting, fretted with sackcloth, fatigued with toil, and dried up with want of sleep; what tho my enemy deride, or rail against, or create me mischief and disquiet; tho cold, or want, or pain, or sickness, wear out a tedious life in sighs and incessant complaints; let my strength be spent in heaviness, and my years in mourning; let me roar for the very anguish of my heart, and my body have no soundness or whole part in it, provided I may find rest in the day of tribulation, and rejoice at last in the felicity of thy chosen, and give thanks with thine inheritance.

For how can we esteem that glory according to its worth, or what can be a purchase equivalent to that happiness in which the face of every righteous man shall shine as the sun in its strength? When the Lord shall reckon up his people, and distribute them into their respective ranks, and the degrees of bliss differing from each other, in proportion to the good they have done in their respective bodies. When he shall put the faithful in possession of those promises they so long depended upon; and in exchange for earthly, give them heavenly, for temporal and transitory, eternal and never fading goods; and make them who have acquitted themselves well in a very little, rulers over much. Nothing sure can be added to the happiness of that day, when the Lord shall introduce his holy ones into his Father's presence, and to make them sit down with himself in heavenly places, that God may be all in all.

O bliss inexpressible, to see the saints, to be with them, to be one of them; to see God as he is, and to possess him for ever and ever! O let this bliss be often in our thoughts, always uppermost, nay, only in our desires: for it deserves the whole of us, and this is the method of insuring it to ourselves. For, if the greatness of the prize put you, as well it may, upon inquiring how you can ever hope to compass it, which way you can deserve it, or what assistances are necessary for this purpose, the answer is short and ready. For God hath so ordained that it is in every man's power to be happy, the kingdom of heaven suffers violence; to desire, and resolve, and endeavor, and strive, is to be qualified, and no man ever failed in his attempt who was willing to take by force.

This kingdom is indeed an invaluable treasure, but yet every man is capable of being a purchaser, because the only price God expects for it is a man's self. Give but yourself, and this will be looked upon as a consideration sufficient. And therefore never be discouraged at the disproportion betwixt what you can pay and what you can hope to receive: for the purchase is paid by another hand to the utmost farthing. This was done when Christ gave himself; and he gave himself that he might ransom you, and make your heart a kingdom for his Father to reign in. Deliver therefore yourself into his possession, that sin may no longer reign in your body unto death, but that God may dwell and reign in you by his Spirit, for the attainment of everlasting life.

How eager then, my soul, should we be to return to that heavenly city, where our home and our privileges are, where we are free

denizens, and have our names enrolled in the
book of God? Since therefore we are fellow
citizens with the saints, heirs of God, and
joint-heirs with Christ, let us very diligently
represent to ourselves the glorious advantages of these characters, and the bliss of our
native place, in the best light our present
thoughts can set them. Let us cry out with
the prophet of old, "How excellent things are
spoken of thee, thou city of God!" All thy
inhabitants are like them that sing, "Beautiful art thou for situation, and the joy of
the whole earth." Into thy gates enter
neither old age, nor decay, nor misery; no
lame or maimed, no deformity or defect, but all
grow up "into a perfect man, unto the measure of the stature of the fulness of Christ."

What can be wanting, what be added, to
the happiness that life, which is never threatened with poverty or sickness, never mo-
lested with wrongs or violence, with anger or
envy, or exorbitant desire; where all the
present necessities of nature cease, and the
restless ambition of honor and power and
riches find no place; where we are no longer
in fear of any devil, or in danger of his temptations, or in so much as a possibility of his
torments; where neither body nor soul can
die, but both are endued with a life everlasting, ever delightful; no casualties, no
malice, no quarrels or factions, but universal

agreement, profound peace, and perfect love; where the day never declines, but a light as perpetual as it is glorious? For "that city hath no need of the sun neither of the moon to shine in it, but the glory of God doth lighten it, and the Lamb is the light thereof," nay, the saints too "shall shine as the brightness of the firmament, and they that turn many to righteousness, as the stars for ever."

Hence there is no night, nor darkness, nor clouds, no extremities of heat and cold, but such a happy temper in all respects as "no eye hath seen, or ear heard, neither hath it entered into the heart of any man to conceive," except those happy souls whom their own experience shall instruct, and whose names are written in the book of life. To all which we may add the honor and happiness of associating with patriarchs and prophets, of conversing with apostles, and martyrs, and saints, and all those dear relations and friends who went thither before us. These are very glorious advantages, but that which far excels them all is that we shall see the face of God, and ever admire and gaze upon and rejoice in his excellent glory. O happiness inestimable, when we shall see God as he is in himself; when we shall see him, and enjoy him ourselves, and when this sight and fruition shall never have any interruption, any end.

The Confessions of St. Augustine

Book One

I

He Declares the Greatness of God, and By Him Arouses Desires to Seek and Call Upon Him

[The "Confessions" of Augustine would in these days be called an "Autobiography." The material is in large part, therefore, historical. The selections which follow comprise practically all of a strictly devotional flavor in the Bishop of Hippo's best-known work.]

"Great art thou, O Lord, and greatly to be praised" (Ps. 145:3); "great is thy power, and thy wisdom is infinite" (Ps. 147:5). And thee would man praise, tho but a fragment of thy creation; man, that bears about him his mortality, that bears about him the witness of his sin, even the witness, that "thou resisteth the proud" (1 Pet. 5:5); yet would man praise thee tho but a fragment of thy creation. Thou dost arouse us to delight in praising thee; for thou hast made us for thyself, and our heart is restless, until it find rest in thee. Grant me, Lord, to know and understand whether to call on thee be the first thing, or to praise thee? and again, whether to know thee or to call on thee? for who can call on thee, that knoweth not thee? for he that knoweth not thee may call on thee as other than thou art. Or, is it rather, that we call on thee that we may know thee? But "how shall they call on him in whom they have not believed? or how shall they believe without a preacher?" (Rom. 10:14); and "they shall praise the Lord that seek him" (Ps. 22:26); for "they that seek shall find him" (Matt. 7:7); and they that find shall praise him. Calling upon thee, Lord, will I seek thee; and believing in thee will I call upon thee; for to us hast thou been preached. My faith, Lord, calls on thee, which thou hast given me, wherewith thou hast inspired me, through the incarnation of thy Son, through the ministry of the preacher.[1]

II

That God, Upon Whom We Call, Is In Us, and We In Him

And how shall I call upon God, my God and Lord? For when I shall call for him, I shall be calling him to myself! and what room is there within me, whither my God may come to me? whither may God come to me, God who

[1] *I.e.*, Ambrose of Milan.

made heaven and earth? is there, indeed, O
Lord my God, aught in me that can contain
thee? do even heaven and earth, which thou
hast made, and wherein thou hast made me,
contain thee? or, since without thee, not anything that is, could be, does it follow that
anything that is doth contain thee? Since,
then, I too am of such a nature, why do I
crave that thou shouldst come to me, who
were not, wert thou not in me? For not yet
am I gone down to hell,, and yet thou art
there also. For "if I go down into hell, thou
art there also" (Ps. 139:7). I could not
then be, O my God, I could not be at all, wert
thou not in me; or is it not rather that I
could not be unless I were in thee, "of whom
are all things, by whom are all things, in
whom are all things?" (Rom. 11:36). Even
so, Lord, even so. Whither do I call thee,
since I am in thee? or whence canst thou come
to me? for whither can I go away beyond
heaven and earth, that thence my God should
come to me, who hath said, "I fill heaven and
earth" (Jer. 23:24).

III

God Wholly Filleth All Things: But Him, Nor Heaven, Nor Earth, Containeth

Do heaven and earth then contain thee, since thou fillest them? or dost thou fill them and yet more of thee remaineth, since they do not contain thee? or whether pourest thou forth what remaineth of thyself when the heaven and earth are full? or hast thou no need that thou by aught shouldst be contained, since thou containest all things, for what thou dost fill by containing thou dost fill? for the vessels which are full of thee uphold thee not, since, tho they were broken, thou wert not poured out. And when thou art "poured out upon us" (Joel 2:28), thou art not thyself cast down, but thou upliftest us; neither art thou scattered, but thou gatherest us. But thou who fillest all things, fillest thou them with thy whole self? or, since all things can not contain thee wholly, do they contain a part of thee? and all at once the same part? or does each contain its own part, the greater more, the smaller less? And is, then, one part of thee greater, another less? or, art thou wholly everywhere, tho naught contains thee wholly?

IV

The Majesty of God Is Supreme: and His Perfections Can Not Be Exprest

What art thou, then, my God? what, I ask, but the Lord God? "For who is Lord but the Lord? or who is God except our God?" (Ps. 18:31, Vulgate). O thou most highest, most good, most potent, most omnipotent; most merciful, yet most just; most hidden, yet most present; fairest, yet most strong; firm, fixt, yet incomprehensible; who changest not, yet changest all things; never new, never old; yet who makest all things new, and "bringest age upon the proud, and they know it not"; ever working, ever at rest; that gatherest, yet lackest nothing; that bearest, and fillest, and coverest; that createst, and nourishest, and makest perfect; that seekest, and yet possessest all things. Thou dost love without passion; thou art jealous, without anxiety; thou repentest without grief; thou art angry without disquiet; thou changest thy works without changing thy purpose; thou receivest again what thou dost find, yet didst never lose; never in need, yet thou rejoicest in gains; never covetous, thou yet demandest usury. Thou receivest over and above that thou mayest owe; and who hath aught that is not thine? Thou payest debts, that owest none; thou forgivest debts, yet losest nothing. And what have I yet said, my God, my life, my holy joy? or what saith any when he speaks of thee? Yet wo to them that speak not of thee, since they that speak most are even as the dumb.

V

He Seeketh Rest In God, and Forgiveness of His Sins

Oh! that I might find rest in thee! Oh! that thou wouldst enter into my heart, and saturate it, that I may forget my own ills, and embrace thee, my only good! What art thou to me? In thy pity, teach me to utter it. Or what am I to thee that thou demandest love from me, and, if I comply not, art wroth with me, and dost menace me with grievous woes? Is it then but a slight wo to love thee not? Ah me! by thy compassions tell me, O Lord my God, what thou art to me. "Say unto my soul, I am thy salvation" (Ps. 35:3). So say it, that I may hear. Behold, Lord, the ears of my heart are before thee; open thou them and "say unto my soul, I am thy salvation." After this word let me hasten and lay hold on thee. Hide not thy face from me. Let me die (that I die not) that I may see thy face.

Narrow is the dwelling-place within my soul; enlarge thou it, that thou mayest enter in. It is ruinous; do thou repair it. It has that within which must offend thine eyes; I confess and know it. But who shall cleanse it? or to whom should I cry, save thee? "Lord, cleanse me from my secret faults; keep thy servant also from presumptuous sins" (Ps. 19:12, 13). "I believe, and therefore do I speak" (Ps. 116:10). Lord, thou knowest. "Have I not confessed my sins unto the Lord: and so thou hast forgiven the wickedness of my sin" (Ps. 32:6). "I contend not in judgment with thee" (Job 9:2), who art the truth; I seek not to deceive myself; "lest mine iniquity lie unto itself" (Ps. 26:12, Vulgate). Therefore I contend not in judgment with thee; "for if thou, Lord, art extreme to mark what is done amiss, O Lord, who may abide it" (Ps. 130:3).

Book Two

VII

He Renders Thanks to God for the Forgiveness of His Sins; and Warns Against Pride Any Whom God Has Kept From Such Grave Offenses

"What shall I render unto the Lord" (Ps. 116:12), that, whilst my memory recalls these things, my soul is not affrighted at them? "I will love thee, O Lord, and give thanks unto thee, and confess unto thy name"; because thou hast forgiven me these so great and wicked deeds of mine. To thy grace I impute it, and to thy mercy, that thou hast melted away my sins as it were ice. To thy grace I impute also that some evil I have left undone; for what might I not have done, who even loved a sin for its own sake? And I confess that all have been forgiven me; both those sins which, of my own will, I did, and those which, of thy guidance, I left undone. What man is there who, conscious of his own infirmity, dares to ascribe his chastity and innocence to his own strength; that so he should love thee the less, as tho thy mercy had been the less necessary for him;

the mercy whereby thou remittest sins to those that turn to thee? For whosoever, called by thee, followed thy voice, and shunned those things which he reads me recording and confessing of myself, let him not scorn me, who being sick, was cured by that Physician, through whose aid it was that he was not sick, or rather was less sick: and for this let him love thee as much, yea and more; since by whom he sees me to have been freed from the weary exhaustion of my sins, by him he sees that he was saved from entanglement in the like exhaustion.

Book Five

I

That It Becomes the Soul To Praise God, and To Confess To Him

Accept the sacrifice of my confessions offered by my tongue, which thou hast formed and stirred up to confess unto thy name. "Heal thou all my bones, and let them say, O Lord, who is like unto thee?" (Ps. 35:10), for he that confesses to thee, doth not inform thee of what is wrought within him; seeing a closed heart can not shut out thine eye, nor can man's hard-heartedness thrust back thy hand; for thou dost melt it, when thou willest, either in pity or in vengeance, "and there is none hid from thy heat" (Ps. 19:6). But let my soul praise thee, that it may love thee; and let it confess to thee thy mercies, that it may praise thee. Thy whole creation ceaseth not thy praises, and is silent never: neither the spirit of every man, by his voice directed toward thee, nor creatures animate or inanimate, by the voice of those who meditate thereon; that so our souls may from their weariness arise toward thee, leaning on those things which thou hast created, and passing on to thyself, who madest them wonderfully; and there is refreshment and true strength.

II

Of the Vanity of Them That Would Escape From God, Seeing He Is Everywhere Present

Let the restless and the unrighteous depart and flee from thee; yet thou seest them, and dividest the darkness; and behold, all things with them are fair, but themselves are foul. And how have they injured thee? or how have they dishonored thy government, which, from the heavens to this lowest earth, is just and perfect? For whither fled

they, when they fled from thy presence? or
where dost not thou find them? But they fled,
that they might not see thee, who seest them,
and, blinded, might stumble against thee; because "thou forsakest nothing thou hast
made" (Wisd. of Sol., 11:25), that the unjust might stumble against thee, and justly
be hurt; withdrawing themselves from thy
gentleness, and stumbling at thy righteousness, and falling upon their own ruggedness.
Indeed, they know not that thou art everywhere, and that no place encloseth thee; and
thou alone art near, even to those that are
far off from thee. Let them then be converted and seek thee; because not as they have
forsaken their Creator, hast thou forsaken thy
creature. Let them be converted and seek
thee; and behold, thou art there in their heart,
in the heart of those that confess to thee, and
cast themselves upon thee, and weep in thy
bosom, after all their rugged ways. Then
dost thou graciously wipe away their tears,
and they weep the more, and joy in weeping;
even for that thou, Lord—not man of flesh
and blood, but—thou, Lord, who madest them,
dost renew them and console them. But
where was I, when I was seeking thee? And
thou wert before me, but I had departed even
from myself; nor did I find myself, how much
less thee!

Book Nine

I

He Praises God for His Goodness In Effecting His Conversion

"O Lord, I am thy servant; I am thy servant, and the son of thy handmaid: thou has broken my bonds in sunder. I will offer to thee the sacrifice of praise" (Ps. 116:17, 18). Let my heart and my tongue praise thee; yea, let "all my bones say, O Lord, who is like unto thee?" (Ps. 35:10). Let them say, and answer thou me, and "say unto my soul, I am thy salvation" (Ps. 35:3). Who am I, and what am I? What of evil have my deeds been without, or if not my deeds, my words, or if not my words, my will? But thou, O Lord, art good and merciful, and thy right hand had respect unto the depth of my death, and from the bottom of my heart didst draw out that abyss of corruption. And this was the whole matter; that I should refuse what I did choose, and choose what thou didst choose. But where throughout that year-long time, and from what low and deep recess was my free-will called forth in a moment, whereby to submit my neck to thy "easy yoke," and my shoulders unto thy "light burden," "O Christ Jesus, my Helper and my Redeemer?" (Matt. 11:30; Ps. 19: 14). How sweet did it at once become to me, to be without sweetness of those toys! and what I feared to lose, I now rejoiced to throw away. For thou didst cast them forth from me, thou true and supreme sweetness. Thou didst cast them forth, and thyself instead didst enter in; who art sweeter than all pleasure, tho not to flesh and blood; brighter than all light, but more inward than any secret place; higher than all honor, but not to them that be high in their own conceits. Now was my soul free from the biting cares of compassing and getting, of wallowing amid and ministering to my lustful foulness; and to thee did I as a child babble, my Light, my Wealth, and my Salvation.

Book Ten

I

He Desireth to Know God

Let me know thee, O my Creator, "let me know thee, even as also I am known" (1 Cor. 13:12). Power of my soul, enter into it, and fit it for thyself, that thou mayest have and hold it "without spot or wrinkle" (Eph. 5:

27). This is my hope, "therefore do I speak" (Ps. 116:10); and in this hope do I rejoice, when I rejoice healthfully. The other things of this life are the less to be bewailed, the more they are bewailed; and the more they are to be bewailed, the less men bewail them. For "behold, thou desirest truth" (Ps. 51:6), and "he that doeth it, cometh to the light" (John 3:20). This would I do in my heart before thee in confession; and in my writing, before many witnesses.

II

Tho God Knoweth the Depths of Our Nature, It Is Good to Make Confession Unto Him

And from thee, O Lord, "in whose eyes is naked" (Heb. 4:13) the abyss of man's conscience, what could be hidden in me tho I were unwilling to confess it? For I should hide thee from myself, not myself from thee. But now, since my groaning beareth witness that I am displeasing to myself, thou shinest out, and art pleasing, and beloved, and longed for; that I may be ashamed of myself, and renounce myself, and choose thee, and neither please thee, nor myself, but in thee. To thee therefore, O Lord, am I open, whatever I am; and with what fruit I confess unto Thee, I have said. Nor do I it with words and utterances of the flesh, but with the words of my soul, and the cry of the thought which thy ear knoweth. For when I am evil, then to confess to thee is nothing else than to be displeased with myself; but when devout, to confess unto thee is nothing else than not to ascribe it to myself: because thou, O Lord, "dost bless the righteous" (Ps. 5:13), but first thou "justifiest him when ungodly" (Rom. 5:10). My confession then, O my God, in thy sight, is made silently, and not silently. For in sound, it is silent; in affection, it cries aloud. For neither do I utter anything right unto men which thou hast not before heard from me; nor dost thou hear any such thing from me, which thou hast not first said unto me.

III

With What Intent He Maketh Confession Before Men of His Present Condition

What then have I to do with men, that they should hear my confessions, as if they could "heal all my infirmities?" (Ps. 103:3). The race is curious to know the lives of others, backward to correct their own. Why seek they to hear from me what I am; who will not hear from thee what themselves are? And how know they, when from myself they hear of myself, whether I say true; seeing "no man knows what is in man, but the spirit of man which is in him?" (1 Cor. 2:11). But if they hear from thee of themselves, they can not say, " The Lord lieth." For what is it to hear from thee of themselves but to know themselves? and who knoweth and saith, "It is false," unless himself lieth? But because "charity believeth all things" (1 Cor. 13:7), especially among those, whom knitting to itself, it maketh one, I also, O Lord, will even so make confession to thee, that men may hear, to whom I am unable to prove whether I confess the truth, yet they whose ears charity openeth to me believe me.

But do thou, my inmost Physician, make plain unto me what fruit I may pluck from this action. For the confessions of my past sins, which thou hast "forgiven and covered" (Ps. 32:1), that thou mightest bless me in thee, changing my soul by faith and thy sacrament, when read and heard, stir up the heart, that it may not slumber in despair, and say, " I can't," but awake in the love of thy mercy and the sweetness of thy grace, whereby, every one that is weak is made strong, when by means of it he becomes conscious within himself of his own weakness, and it delighteth the good to hear the past sins of them that now have abandoned them; but it delights them not because they are evil, but because they were, and are so no longer. With what fruit then, O Lord my God, to whom day by day my conscience confesseth, trusting rather in the hope of thy mercy than in its own innocence, with what fruit, I ask, do I, by this book, confess to men also in thy presence, what I now am, not what I have been? For that other fruit I have seen and described. But what I now am, at the very time of making these confessions, many desire to know, who have or have not known me, who have heard from me or of me; but their ear is not at my heart, where I am, whatever I am. They wish then to hear me confess what I am within; whither they can penetrate neither with eye, nor ear, nor mind; they are even willing to believe; but will they know? For charity, whence they gain their goodness, telleth them that in my confessions I lie not; and she in them, believeth me.

IV

He Declares What Results He Hopeth for From His Confessions

But for what fruit do they desire this? Are they desirous to rejoice with me when they have heard how near to thee I draw by thy bounty, and to pray for me when they have heard how much I am hindered by my own weight? To such will I discover myself. For it is no small fruit, O Lord my God, "that by many thanks should be given to thee on our behalf" (2 Cor. 1:11), and that thou shouldst be entreated by many for us. Let the fraternal spirit love in me what thou teachest is to be loved, and lament in me what thou teachest is to be lamented. This let a fraternal spirit do, not a stranger's, not that of the "strange children, whose mouth talketh of vanity, and their right hand is a right hand of iniquity" (Ps. 144:11), but that fraternal spirit which, when it approveth me, rejoiceth for me, and when it disapproveth me, sorroweth for me; because whether it approveth or disapproveth, it loveth me. To such will I discover myself; at that which is good in me let them draw breath with joy, at what is ill let them breathe a sigh. All my good is thy appointment, and thy gift; all my evil mine own faults and thy judgments. For the one let them draw breath with joy, for the other let them sigh—and let their hymn and their lamentation both ascend into thy presence from their fraternal hearts, which are thy censors. But do thou, O Lord, rejoicing in the sweet perfume of thy holy temple, "have mercy upon me after thy great goodness" (Ps. 51), for thy name's sake; and by no means forsaking what thou hast begun, make perfect my imperfections.

This is the fruit of my confessions, not of what I have been, but of what I am, that I may confess this not only before thee, with a secret "rejoicing with trembling" (Ps. 2:11), and a secret sorrowing with hope, but also in the ears of the sons of men who believe, the companions of my joy and partakers of my mortality, fellow citizens and fellow pilgrims with me, whether they are gone before or follow after or tread with me the path of life. These are thy servants, my brethren, whom thou hast willed to be thy

sons; my masters, whom thou has bidden me
serve, if I would live with thee, of thee. But
this thy word were all too little for me, did
it in speech alone enjoin, and not in deed
prevent. And this I do both in deeds and
words, this I do "beneath thy wings" in peril
too great, were not my soul subdued to thee
beneath thy wings, and my weakness known
to thee. I am but a little one, but my Father
ever liveth, and my Guardian is "sufficient
for me." For he is the same who hath begotten and doth guard me; and thou thyself
art all my good; thou Almighty, who art
with me, yea, before I am with thee. To such
then as thou biddest me serve, will I discover
not what I have been, but what I now am
and what I yet may be. But yet "I judge
not mine own self" (1 Cor. 4:3). Thus
therefore I would be heard.

V

Our Confessions Can Not But Be Imperfect; for Man Knoweth Not Himself as God Knoweth

For "thou, Lord, dost judge me" because, altho "no man knoweth the things
of a man, but the spirit of a man which is in
him," yet is there something of man, which

not even "the spirit of man that is in him," itself "knoweth" (1 Cor. 2 : 11). But thou, Lord, who hast made him, knowest all concerning him. Yet I, tho in thy sight I despise myself, and account myself "dust and ashes"; yet know I something of thee, which I know not of myself. And in truth "now we see through a glass darkly," not yet "face to face" (1 Cor. 13 : 12); and therefore so long as I wander far off from thee, I am more present with myself than with thee; and yet I know that thou canst in no way suffer harm. But what temptations I can resist, what I can not, I know not. Yet there is hope, because "thou art faithful, who wilt not suffer us to be tempted above that we are able; but wilt with the temptation also make a way to escape, that we may be able to bear it" (1 Cor. 10 : 13). I will confess then what I know of myself, I will confess also what I know not of myself; since what I do know of myself, I know by thy shining upon me; and what I know not of myself, I know not only until "my darkness be made as the noon-day" (Isa. 58 : 10) in thy countenance.

XXII

The True Story of the Blessed Life

Far be it, Lord, far be it from the heart of thy servant who here confesseth unto thee, far be it, that, be the joy what it may, I should therefore think myself happy. For there is a "joy" which is "not" given "to the ungodly" (Isa. 48:22), but to those who worship thee for thine own sake, whose joy thou thyself art. And this is the blessed life, to rejoice to thee, of thee, for thee; this it is, and there is no other. For they who think there is another, pursue some other joy, and not the true. But their will is not turned away from some shadow of joy.

XXIII

That All Desire Joy In the Truth

It is not certain then that all wish to be happy, inasmuch as they who wish not to joy in thee, which is the only blessed life, do not truly desire the blessed life. Or do all men desire this, but "because the flesh lusteth against the Spirit, and the Spirit against

the flesh, so that they can not do the things
that they would'' (Gal. 5:17), they fall upon
that which they can, and are content there-
with; because, what they are not able to do,
they do not will so strongly, as would suffice to
make them able? For I ask any one, had he
rather joy in truth, or in falsehood? They
will as little hesitate to say, ''in the truth,''
as to say, ''that they desire to be happy.''
But the blessed life is joy in the truth. For
this is a joying in thee, who art ''the truth,''
O God ''my light, health of my countenance,
my God'' (Ps. 27:1; 42:11). This blessed
life all desire; this life, which alone is blessed,
all desire; joy in the truth all desire. I have
met with many that would fain deceive; who
would choose to be deceived? no one. Where
then did they know this happy life, save
where they knew the truth also? For they
love it also, since they would not be deceived.
And when they love a happy life, which is no
other than rejoicing in the truth, then also
do they love the truth; but they could not love
it, were there not some notice of it in their
memory. Why then do they not rejoice in
it? why are they not happy? because they are
more strongly taken up with other things
which have more power to make them miserable, than with that which they so faintly remember to make them happy. For there is

yet a little light in men; let them walk, "let them walk, lest darkness come upon them" (John 12:35).

But why doth "truth bring forth hatred," and why is that man of thine that preacheth truth become their enemy, seeing that the blessed life is loved, which is nothing else than rejoicing in the truth; unless it be that truth is loved only in such a sort that they who love something else than it want what they love to be the truth; and because they are unwilling to be deceived, are unwilling to be convinced that they have been deceived? Therefore, for the sake of that thing, which instead of truth they love, they hate the truth. They love her when she enlightens; but they hate her when she rebukes. For since they would not be deceived, and would deceive, they love her when she manifests herself, but hate her when she manifests them. Whence she shall so repay them, that they who would not be made manifest by her, she both against their will makes manifest and herself becometh not manifest unto them. Thus, thus, yea thus doth the mind of man, thus blind and sick, foul and ill-favored, wish to be hidden, but that aught should be hidden from it it wills not. But the contrary is requited it, that itself should not be hidden from the truth; but the truth is hid from it. Yet

even thus whilst wretched, it would rather
rejoice in truths than in falsehoods. Happy
then will it be, when, no distraction inter-
posing, it shall rejoice in that one truth, by
which all things are true.

XLIII

The Man Christ Jesus the Only Mediator Between God and Man. In Him His Soul Is Satisfied

But the true Mediator, whom in thy secret
mercy thou hast shewed to the humble, and
didst send that by his example also they might
learn the same humility, that "Mediator between God and man, the man Christ Jesus"
(1 Tim. 2:5), appeared betwixt mortal sinners and the immortal Just One; sharing with
men mortality, with God righteousness: so
that since the wages of righteousness is life
and peace, he might by a righteousness con-
joined with God make void that death of justified sinners, which it was his will to share
in common with them. Hence he was shewed
forth to holy men of old; that they too through
faith in his passion to come, as we through
faith in it past, might be saved. In so far

as he was man, he was a Mediator; in that he was the Word, he was not in a middle place, because equal with God, and God with God, and together (with the Holy Spirit) one God.

How hast thou loved us, O good Father, who "sparedst not thine only Son, but deliveredst him up for us ungodly!" (Rom. 8:32). How hast thou loved us, for whom, "he that thought it not robbery to be equal with thee, was made subject even to the death of the cross" (Phil. 2:6). He alone "free among the dead" (Ps. 88:5), "having power to lay down his life, and power to take it again" (John 10:18): for us to thee both Victor and Victim, and therefore Victor, because the Victim; for us to thee Priest and Sacrifice, and therefore Priest because the Sacrifice; making us to thee sons instead of servants, by being begotten of thee, and becoming servant to us. Rightly then is my hope strong in him, that thou "wilt heal all my infirmities" by him who "sitteth at thy right hand and maketh intercession for us" (Rom. 8:34), otherwise I should despair. For many and great are those infirmities of mine, many they are, and great; but thy medicine is greater. We might think that thy Word was far removed from any union with man, and despair of ourselves, had he not been "made flesh and dwelt among us" (John 1:14).

Affrighted with my sins and the burden of my misery, I had devised in my heart, and purposed to "flee to the wilderness"; but thou didst forbid me, and strengthen me, saying, "Therefore Christ died for all, that they which live should not henceforth live unto themselves, but unto him which died for them" (2 Cor. 5:15). See, Lord, I "cast my care upon thee" that I may live, and I will "consider the wondrous things of thy law" (Ps. 119:18). Thou knowest my unskilfulness, and my weakness; teach me, and heal me. He, thine only Son, "in whom are hid all the treasures of wisdom and knowledge" (Col. 2:3), hath redeemed me with his blood. "Let not the proud speak evil of me"; because I think upon the price of my Redemption, and eat and drink, and communicate it; and being "poor," I desire to be satisfied from him amongst those who "eat and are satisfied. And they shall praise the Lord that seek him" (Ps. 20:26).

SELECTIONS FROM

The Sermons of Leo the Great

BISHOP OF ROME

FROM THE TRANSLATION

BY

REV. CHARLES LETT FELTOE, M.A.

Nicene and Post-Nicene Fathers

SECOND SERIES, VOL. XII.

LEO I. (THE GREAT)

Was born in Tuscany and the year of his birth is unknown. He died November 10, 461. He succeeded Sixtus as pope in 440. He was an uncompromising foe of heresy. In the year 444 he laid down the principle that Peter had received the primacy and oversight of the whole Church as a requital of his faith and that thus all important matters were to be referred to and decided by Rome. At one time, when he felt that "the Roman universal monarchy was threatened, he appealed to the civil power for support and obtained from Valentinian III. the famous decree of June 6, 445, which recognized the primacy of the bishop of Rome, based on the merits of Peter, the dignity of the city, and the decrees of Nicæa (in their interpolated form); ordained that any opposition to his rulings, which were to have the force of law, should be treated as treason; and provided for the forcible extradition by provincial governors of anyone who refused to answer a summons to Rome." According to Leo, the Church is built upon Peter, in keeping with the promise made in Matt. 16:16-19. "When Attila invaded Italy in 452 and threatened Rome, it was Leo who, with two high civil functionaries, went to meet him, and so imprest him that he withdrew. His intercession could not prevent the sack of the city by Genseric in 455, but murder and arson were represt by his influence." The English translation of selected letters and sermons is given in the "Nicene and Post-Nicene Fathers," 2d Series, Vol. XII.

On the Feast of the Tenth Month

[THAT IS, OF THE ADVENT SEASON]

1. Restoration to the divine image in which we were made is possible only by our imitation of God's will. If, dearly beloved, we comprehended faithfully and wisely the beginning of our creation, we shall find that man was made in God's image, to the end that he might imitate his Creator, and that our race attains its highest natural dignity, by the form of the Divine goodness being reflected in us as in a mirror. And assuredly to this form the Savior's grace is daily restoring us, so long as that which in the first Adam fell is raised up again in the second. And the cause of our restoration is naught else but the mercy of God, whom we should not have loved unless he had first loved us and dispelled the darkness of our ignorance by the light of his truth. And the Lord foretelling this by the holy Isaiah says, "I will bring the blind into a way that they knew not, and will make them walk in paths which they were ignorant of. I will turn darkness into light for them, and the crooked into the straight. These things will I do for

By kind permission of Charles Scribner's Sons.

them and not forsake them'' (Isa. 42:16,
and 65:1). And again he says, ''I was
found by them that sought me not, and openly
appeared to them that asked not for me''
(Isa. 42:16, and 65:1). And the Apostle
John teaches us how this has been fulfilled
when he says, ''We know that the Son of God
is come, and has given us an understanding,
that we may know him that is true, and may
be in him that is true, even his Son'' (1 John
5:20, and 4:19), and again, ''Let us therefore love God, because he first loved us'' (1
John 5:20, and 4:19). Thus it is that God, by
loving us, restores us to his image, and, in
order that he may find in us the form of his
goodness, he gives us that whereby we ourselves too may do the work that he does,
kindling that is the lamps of our minds, and
inflaming us with the fire of his love that
we may love not only himself but also whatever he loves. For if between men that is
the lasting friendship which is based upon
similarity of character, notwithstanding that
such identity of wills is often directed to
wicked ends, how ought we to yearn and
strive to differ in nothing from what is pleasing to God. Of which the prophet speaks,
''for wrath is in his indignation, and life
in his pleasure'' (Ps. 30:5, Septuagint),
because we shall not otherwise attain the

dignity of the divine Majesty, unless we imitate his will.

2. We must love both God and our neighbor, and "our neighbor" must be interpreted in its widest sense. And so, when the Lord says, "Thou shalt love the Lord thy God from all thy heart and from all thy mind; and thou shalt love thy neighbor as thyself" (Matt. 22: 37, 39), let the faithful soul put on the unfading love of its Author and Ruler, and subject itself also entirely to his will in whose works and judgments true justice and tender-hearted compassion never fail. For altho a man be wearied out with labors and many misfortunes, there is good reason for him to endure all in the knowledge that adversity will either prove him good or make him better. But this godly love can not be perfect unless a man love his neighbor also. Under which name must be included not only those who are connected with us by friendship or neighborhood, but absolutely all men, with whom we have a common nature whether they be foes or allies, slaves or free. For the one Maker fashioned us, the one Creator breathed life into us; we all enjoy the same sky and air, the same days and nights, and, tho some be good others bad, some righteous others unrighteous, yet God is bountiful to all, kind to all, as Paul

and Barnabas said to the Lycaonians concerning God's providence: "Who in generations gone by suffered all the nations to walk in their own ways. And yet he left himself not without witness, doing them good, giving rain from heaven, and fruitful seasons, and filling our hearts with food and gladness" (Acts 14:16, 17). But the wide extent of Christian grace has given us yet greater reasons for loving our neighbor, which, reaching to all parts of the whole world, looks down on no one and teaches that no one is to be neglected. And full rightly does he command us to love our enemies and to pray to him for our persecutors, who, daily grafting shoots of the wild olive from among all nations, upon the holy branches of his own olive, makes men reconciled instead of enemies, adopted sons instead of strangers, just instead of ungodly, "that every knee may bow of things in heaven, of things on earth, and of things under the earth, and every tongue confess that the Lord Jesus Christ is the glory of God the Father" (Phil. 2:10, 11).

3. We must be thankful and show our thankfulness for what we have received, whether much or little. Accordingly, as God wishes us to be good, because he is good, none of his judgments ought to displease us. For

not to give him thanks in all things—what else is it but to blame him in some degree. Man's folly too often dares to murmur against his Creator, not only in time of want, but also in time of plenty; so that when something is not supplied he complains, and when certain things are in abundance he is ungrateful. The lord of rich harvests thought scorn of his well-filled garners, and groaned over his abundant grape-gathering; he did not give thanks for the size of the crop, but complained of its poorness (Luke 12:16-20). And if the ground has been less prolific than its wont in the seed it has reared, and the vines and the olives have failed in their supply of fruit, the year is accused, the elements blamed, neither the air nor the sky is spared, whereas nothing better befits and reassures the faithful and godly disciples of truth than the persistent and unwearied lifting of praise to God, as says the apostle: "Rejoice alway, pray without ceasing; in all things give thanks. For this is the will of God in Christ Jesus in all things for you" (1 Thess. 5:16). But how shall we be partakers of this devotion unless vicissitudes of fortune train our minds in constancy, so that the love directed toward God may not be puffed up in prosperity nor faint in adversity. Let that which pleased God please us too. Let us rejoice

in whatever measure of gifts he gives. Let
him who has used great possessions well, use
small ones also well. Plenty and scarcity
may be equally for our own good, and even
in spiritual progress we shall not be cast down
at the smallness of the results, if our minds
become not dry and barren. Let that spring
from the soil of our heart which the earth
gave not. To him that fails not in good will
means to give are ever supplied. Therefore,
dearly beloved, in all works of godliness let
us use what each year gives us, and let
not seasons of difficulty hinder our Christian
benevolence. The Lord knows how to re-
plenish the widow's vessels, which her pious
deed of hospitality has emptied; he knows
how to turn water into wine: he knows how
to satisfy 5,000 hungry persons with a few
loaves. And he who is fed in his poor can
multiply when he takes what he increased
when he gave.

4. Prayer, fasting and almsgiving are the
three comprehensive duties of a Christian.
But there are three things which most belong
to religious actions, namely, prayer, fasting,
and almsgiving, in the exercising of which,
while every time is accepted, yet that ought
to be more zealously observed which we have
received as hallowed by tradition from the
apostles: even as this month brings round

again to us the opportunity when according to the ancient practise we may give more diligent heed to those three things of which I have spoken. For by prayer we seek to propitiate God, by fasting we extinguish the lusts of the flesh, by alms we redeem our sins; and at the same time God's image is throughout renewed in us, if we are always ready to praise him, unfailingly intent on our purification and unceasingly active in cherishing our neighbor. This threefold round of duty, dearly beloved, brings all other virtues into action: it attains to God's image and likeness and unites us inseparably with the Holy Spirit. Because in prayer faith remains stedfast, in fastings life remains innocent, and in almsgiving the mind remains kind. On Wednesday and Friday therefore let us fast: and on Saturday let us keep vigil with the most blessed Apostle Peter, who will deign to aid our supplications and fast and alms with his own prayers through our Lord Jesus Christ, who with the Father and the Holy Ghost lives and reigns for ever and ever. AMEN.

On the Feast of the Nativity

1. Christmas morning is the most appropriate time for thoughts on the Nativity. On all days and at all times, dearly beloved, does the birth of our Lord and Savior from the virgin mother occur to the thoughts of the faithful who meditate on divine things, that the mind may be aroused to the acknowledgment of its Maker, and whether it be occupied in the groans of supplication, or in the shouting of praise, or in the offering of sacrifice, may employ its spiritual insight on nothing more frequently and more trustingly than on the fact that God the Son of God, begotten of the co-eternal Father, was also born by a human birth. But this nativity which is to be adored in heaven and on earth is suggested to us by no day more than this when, with the early light still shedding its rays on nature, there is borne in upon our senses the brightness of this wondrous mystery. For the angel Gabriel's converse with the astonished Mary and her conception by the Holy Ghost, as wondrously promised as believed, seem to occur not only to the memory but to the very eyes. For to-day the Maker of the world was born of a Virgin's womb, and he, who made all natures, became Son of her whom he created. To-day the

Word of God appeared clothed in flesh, and that which had never been visible to human eyes began to be tangible to our hands as well. To-day the shepherds learned from the angels' voices that the Savior was born in the substance of our flesh and soul; and to-day the form of the gospel message was prearranged by the leaders of the Lord's flocks, so that we too may say with the army of the heavenly host: "Glory in the highest to God, and on earth peace to men of good will."

2. Christians are essentially participators in the nativity of Christ. Altho, therefore, that infancy, which the majesty of God's Son did not disdain, reached mature manhood by the growth of years, and when the triumph of his passion and resurrection was completed, all the actions of humility which were undertaken for us ceased, yet to-day's festival renews for us the holy childhood of Jesus born of the Virgin Mary; and in adoring the birth of our Savior, we find we are celebrating the commencement of our own life, for the birth of Christ is the source of life for Christian folk, and the birthday of the Head is the birthday of the body. Altho every individual that is called has his own order. and all the sons of the Church are separated from one another by intervals of time, yet

as the entire body of the faithful being born
in the font of baptism is crucified with Christ
in his passion, raised again in his resurrection, and placed at the Father's right hand
in his ascension, so with him are they born
in this nativity. For any believer in whatever
part of the world that is reborn in Christ
quits the old paths of his original nature
and passes into a new man by being reborn;
and no longer is he reckoned of his earthly
father's stock but among the seed of the
Savior, who became the Son of man in order
that we might have the power to be the sons
of God. For unless he came down to us in
this humiliation, no one would reach his presence by any merits of his own. Let not
earthly wisdom shroud in darkness the hearts
of the called on this point and let not the
frailty of earthly thoughts raise itself against
the loftiness of God's grace, for it will soon
return to the lowest dust. At the end of
the ages is fulfilled that which was ordained
from all eternity, and in the presence of
realities, when signs and types have ceased,
the law and prophecy have become truth
and so Abraham is found the father of all
nations, and the promised blessing is given
to the world in his seed: nor are they only
Israelites whom blood and flesh (Heb. 2: 14)
begot, but the whole body of the adopted en

ter into possession of the heritage prepared for the sons of faith. Be not disturbed by the cavils of silly questionings, and let not the effects of the divine word be dissipated by human calculation; we with Abraham believe in God and "waver not through unbelief" (Rom. 4: 20, 21), but "know most assuredly that what the Lord promised he is able to perform."

3. Peace with God is his best gift to man. The Savior then, dearly beloved, is born not of fleshly seed but of the Holy Spirit, in such wise that the condemnation of the first transgression did not touch him. And hence the very greatness of the boon conferred demands of us reverence worthy of its splendor. For, as the blessed apostle teaches, "we have received not the spirit of this world but the spirit which is of God, that we may know the things which are given us by God" (1 Cor. 2: 12), and that Spirit can in no other way be rightly worshiped except by offering him that which we received from him. But in the treasures of the Lord's bounty what can we find so suitable to the honor of the present feast as the peace which at the Lord's nativity was first proclaimed by the angel choir? For that it is which brings forth the sons of God, the nurse of love and the mother of unity, the rest of

the blessed and our eternal home; whose proper work and special office it is to join to God those whom it removes from the world. Whence the apostle incites us to this good end in saying, "being justified therefore by faith, let us have peace towards God" (Rom. 5:1). In which brief sentence are summed up nearly all the commandments; for where true peace is, there can be no lack of virtue. But what is it, dearly beloved, to have peace toward God, except to wish what he bids, and not to wish what he forbids? For if human friendships seek out equality of soul and similarity of desires, and difference of habits can never attain to full harmony, how will he be partaker of divine peace who is pleased with what displeases God, and desires to get delight from what he knows to be offensive to God? That is not the spirit of the sons of God; such wisdom is not acceptable to the noble family of the adopted. That chosen and royal race must live up to the dignity of its regeneration, must love what the Father loves and in nought disagree with its Maker, lest the Lord should again say: "I have begotten and raised up sons, but they have scorned me: the ox knoweth his owner, and the ass his master's crib: but Israel hath not known me, and my people hath not acknowledged me" (Isa. 1:2, 3).

4. We must be worthy of our calling as sons and friends of God. The mystery of this boon is great, dearly beloved, and this gift exceeds all gifts, that God should call man son and man should name God Father: for by these terms we perceive and learn the love which reached so great a height. For if in natural progeny and earthly families those who are born of noble parents are lowered by the faults of evil intercourse, and unworthy offspring are put to shame by the very brilliance of their ancestry; to what end will they come who through love of the world do not fear to be outcast from the family of Christ? But if it gains the praise of men that the father's glory should shine again in their descendants, how much more glorious is it for those who are born of God to regain the brightness of their Maker's likeness and display in themselves him who begat them, as saith the Lord: "Let your light so shine before men that they may see your good works and glorify your Father which is in heaven" (Matt. 5:16). We know indeed, as the Apostle John says, that "the whole world lieth in the evil one" (1 John 5:19), and that by the stratagems of the devil and his angels numberless attempts are made either to frighten man in his struggle upward by adversity or to spoil him by pros-

perity, but "greater is he that is with us than he that is against us" (1 John 4:4, and 2 Kings 6:16), and they who have peace with God and are always saying to the Father with their whole hearts "thy will be done" (Matt. 6:10) can be overcome in no battles, can be hurt by no assaults. For accusing ourselves in our confessions and refusing the spirit's consent to our fleshly lusts, we stir up against us the enmity of him who is the author of sin, but secure a peace with God that nothing can destroy, by accepting his gracious service, in order that we may not only surrender ourselves in obedience to our King but also be united to him by our free-will. For if we are like-minded, if we wish what he wishes and disapprove what he disapproves, he will finish all our wars for us, he who gave the will will also give the power: so that we may be fellow workers in his works, and with the exultation of faith may utter that prophetic song: "The Lord is my light and my salvation: whom shall I fear? The Lord is the defender of my life: of whom shall I be afraid?" (Ps. 27:1).

5. The birth of Christ is the birth of peace to the Church. They then who "are born not of blood nor of the will of the flesh nor of the will of man but of God" (John 1:13) must offer to the Father the unanimity

of peace-loving sons, and all the members of adoption must meet in the First-Begotten of the new creation, who came to do not his own will but his that sent him; inasmuch as the Father in his gracious favor has adopted as his heirs not those that are discordant nor those that are unlike him, but those that are in feeling and affection one. They that are remodeled after one pattern must have a spirit like the model. The birthday of the Lord is the birthday of peace: for thus says the apostle, "He is our peace who made both one" (Eph. 2:14, 18); since whether we be Jew or Gentile, "through him we have access in one Spirit to the Father" (Eph. 2:14, 18). And it was this in particular that he taught his disciples before the day of his passion which he had of his own free-will foreordained, saying, "My peace I give unto you, my peace I leave for you" (John 14:27); and lest under the general term the character of his peace should escape notice, he added, "not as the world give I unto you" (John 14:27). The world, he says, has its friendships, and brings many that are apart into loving harmony. There are also minds which are equal in vices, and similarity of desires produces equality of affection. And if any are perchance to be found who are not pleased with what is mean and dishonorable, and who exclude from the terms of their connection unlawful compacts, yet even such, if they be either Jews, heretics, or heathens, belong not to God's friendship but to this world's peace. But the peace of the spiritual and of catholics coming down from above and leading upward refuses to hold communion with the lovers of the world, resists all obstacles, and flies from pernicious pleasures to true joys, as the Lord says: "Where thy treasure is, there will thy heart be also" (Matt. 6:21): that is, if what you love is below, you will descend to the lowest depth; if what you love is above, you will reach the topmost height. Thither may the Spirit of peace lead and bring us, whose wishes and feeling are at one, and who are of one mind in faith and hope and in charity; since "as many as are led by the Spirit of God these are sons of God" (Rom. 8:14), who reigneth with the Son and Holy Spirit for ever and ever. AMEN.

SELECTIONS FROM

The Proslogium

BY

ST. ANSELM

FROM THE TRANSLATION

BY

J. S. MAGINNIS, D.D.

ST. ANSELM OF CANTERBURY

Father of medieval scholasticism and one of the most eminent of English prelates; born at Oasta, Piedmont, 1033; died at Canterbury, England, April 21, 1109. At the age of fifteen Anselm desired to enter the monastic life, but his father opposed the idea. He studied at the monastery of Bec in Normandy, under Lanfranc, and succeeded his master as prior, and in 1078 became abbot of this monastery. He was appointed archbishop of Canterbury in succession to Lanfranc in 1093. "In. the history of theology he stands as the father of orthodox scholasticism," and has been called the Second Augustine. His most celebrated works are the "Monologium" and the "Proslogium," both aiming to prove the nature and existence of God, and the "Cur Deus Homo," in which he develops views of atonement and satisfaction which are still held by the orthodox theologians. Besides the philosophical treatises there are his "Meditations" and "Letters."

O, vain man! flee now, for a little while from thine accustomed occupations; hide thyself for a brief moment from thy tumultuous thoughts; cast aside thy cares; postpone thy toilsome engagements; devote thyself awhile to God; repose for a moment in him; enter into the sanctuary of thy soul, exclude thence all else but God, and whatever may aid thee in finding him; then, within the closed doors of thy retirement, inquire after thy God. Say now, O my whole heart! say now to thy God: I seek thy face; thy face O Lord do I seek. Therefore now, O Lord, my God, teach thou my heart where and how it may seek for thee; where and how it may find thee. If thou art not here, O Lord, where, while thou art absent, shall I find thee? But if thou art everywhere, why do I not see thee present? Truly thou dwellest in light inaccessible! But where is this inaccessible light, or how can I approach to light inaccessible? Who will lead me and conduct me into it, that I may behold thee there? And then by what signs, or under what form shall I seek thee? I have never seen thee, O Lord my God; I know not thy face. What shall this thine exile do—O Lord, thou Most High, what shall he do, banished so far from thee? What shall thy servant do, cast far away from thy presence, and yet in anguish with love for thy perfections? He pants to see thee, but thy face is too far from him; he desires to approach unto thee, but thy habitation is inaccessible; he longs to find thee, but knows not thine abode. He attempts to seek thee, but knows not thy face. O Lord, thou art my Lord and my God, but as yet I have never seen thee. Thou hast created and redeemed me, and hast conferred upon me all my goods, but I know thee not. In fine, I was created that I might behold thee; but I have not yet attained to the end of my creation. O miserable lot of man, since he has lost that for which he was created! O hard and cruel misfortune! Alas! what has he lost and what has he found? What has departed and what remains? He has lost the blessedness for which he was created; he has found misery for which he was not created. That has departed, without which there is no happiness; that remains, which, in itself, is naught but misery. Then man was accustomed to eat the bread of angels, for which he now hungers; now he eats the bread of sorrows, of which he was then ignorant. Alas! the common affliction of man, the universal wailing of the sons of Adam! The father of our race was filled to satiety, we pine, from hunger; he abounded, we are in want; he possest happiness, but miserably deserted it; we are destitute of happiness, and pitifully long for it; but alas! our desires are unsatisfied. Why, since he could easily have done it, did he not preserve for us that which we should so greatly need? Why did he thus exclude from us the light and surround us with darkness? Why has he deprived us of life and inflicted death? Miserable beings! Whence have we been expelled? Whither are we driven? From what heights have we been precipitated? Into what abyss are we plunged? From our native land into exile; from the presence of God into the darkness which now envelops us; from the sweets of immortality into the bitterness and horror of death. Unhappy change—from good so great to evil so enormous! O heavy loss! heavy grief! heavy all! But alas! wretch that I am, miserable son of Eve, estranged from God, at what did I aim? What have I accomplished? Whither did I direct my course? Where have I arrived? To what did I aspire? For what do I now sigh? I sought for good, but behold confusion and trouble! I attempted to go to God, but I only stumbled upon myself. In my retirement I

sought for rest, but in the depths of my heart
I found tribulation and anguish. I desired to
laugh by reason of the joy of my mind, but
I am compelled to roar by reason of the dis-
quietude of my heart. I hoped for happiness,
but behold! from this my sighs are multiplied. And thou, O Lord, how long? How
long O Lord wilt thou forget us? How long
wilt thou turn thy face from us? When wilt
thou have respect unto us and hear us? When
wilt thou enlighten our eyes and show us thy
face? When wilt thou restore thyself unto
us? Have respect unto us, O Lord hear us,
enlighten us, show thyself to us. Restore
thyself unto us, that it may be well with us;
it is so ill with us without thee. Have pity
upon our toils and our efforts after thee; we
can do nothing without thee. Invite us; aid
us; I beseech thee, O Lord, let me not despair
in my longing; but let me be refreshed by
hope. My heart is embittered in its own
desolation; assuage thou its sorrows by thy
consolations. O Lord, opprest with hunger
I have commenced to seek thee; let me not
cease till I am filled from thy bounty; fam-
ished, I have approached unto thee; let me not
depart unfed; poor, I have come to thy riches;
miserable, to thy compassion; let me not return empty and despised. And if, before I
partake of this divine food, I long for it,

grant after my desires are excited that I may have sufficient to satisfy them. O Lord I am bowed down and can look only toward the earth; raise thou me, that I may look upward. Mine iniquities have gone over my head; they cover me over, and as a heavy burden they bear me down. Set me free; deliver me from mine iniquities, lest their pit shall close upon me its mouth. Let me behold thy light, whether from the depth or from the distance. Teach me to seek thee; and while I seek show thyself to me; because, unless thou teach, I can not seek thee; unless thou show thyself, I can not find thee; let me seek thee by desiring thee; let me desire thee by seeking thee. Let me find thee by loving thee; let me love thee in finding thee. I confess, O Lord, and render thee thanks that thou hast created in me this thine image, that I may be mindful of thee, that I may contemplate and love thee; but it is so injured by contact with vice, so darkened by the vapor of sin, that it can not attain to that for which it was created, unless thou wilt renew and reform it. I attempt not to penetrate to thy height, for with this my feeble intelligence can bear no comparison; but I desire, in some degree, to understand thy truth which my heart believes and loves. For I seek not to understand in order that I may believe; but I believe in order that I may understand, for I believe for this reason that unless I believe I can not understand.

That God Truly Exists, Altho the Fool Hath Said In His Heart, There Is No God

Therefore, O Lord, thou who dost impart understanding to faith, grant, so far as thou seest this knowledge would be expedient for me, that I may know that thou art as we believe, and that thou art this which we believe. And, indeed, we believe that thou art something, than which nothing greater can be conceived. Shall we, therefore, conclude that there is no such being, merely because the fool hath said in his heart, there is no God? But surely even this same fool, when he hears me announce that there is something than which nothing greater can be conceived, understands what he hears, and what he understands is in his conception, even if he does not know that it exists. For, it is one thing for an object to be in the conception, and another to know that it exists. For when the painter conceives, beforehand, the picture which he is about to sketch, he has it, indeed, in his conception; but he knows that it does not yet exist, for he has not as yet executed it. But, after he has painted, he not only has in his conception what he has just produced, but he knows that it exists. Even the fool, therefore, is convinced that there exists in his conception something than which nothing greater can be conceived; because, when he hears this mentioned, he understands it, or forms an idea of it, and whatever is understood is in the intelligence. And surely that than which a greater can not be conceived can not exist in the intelligence alone. For, let it be supposed that it exists only in the intelligence; then something greater can be conceived, for it can be conceived to exist in reality also, which is greater. If, therefore, that than which a greater can not be conceived, exists in the conception or intelligence alone, then that very thing, than which a greater can not be conceived, is something than which a greater can be conceived, which is impossible. There exists, therefore, beyond doubt, both in the intelligence and in reality, something than which a greater can not be conceived.

That God Can Not Be Conceived Not to Exist

Indeed, so truly does this exist, that it can not be conceived not to exist. For it is possible to conceive of the existence of something which can not be conceived not to exist; and this is greater than that which can be conceived not to exist. Wherefore, if that, than which a greater can not be conceived, can be conceived not to exist, then this something, than which a greater can not be conceived, is something than which a greater can be conceived; which is a contradiction. So truly, therefore, does something exist, than which a greater can not be conceived, that it is impossible to conceive this not to exist. And this art thou, O Lord our God! So truly, therefore, dost thou exist, O Lord my God, that thou canst not be conceived not to exist. For this there is the highest reason. For if any mind could conceive of anything better than thou art, then the creature could ascend above the Creator, and become his judge; which is supremely absurd. Everything else, indeed, which exists besides thee can be conceived not to exist. Thou alone, therefore, of all things, hast being in the truest sense, and consequently in the highest degree; for everything else that is exists not so truly, and has, consequently, being only in an inferior degree. Why, therefore, has the fool said in his heart, there is no God? since it is so manifest to an intelligent mind, that of all things thine existence is the highest reality. Why, unless because he is a fool, and destitute of reason?

How and Why God Is Seen and Not Seen By Those Who Seek Him

Hast thou found, O my soul, what thou wast seeking? Thou wast seeking God, thou hast found him to be something supreme over all, than which nothing more excellent can be conceived; that this is life itself, light, wisdom, goodness, eternal blessedness, and blessed eternity; and that this is everywhere and always. For if thou hast not found thy God, then he must be something different from that which thou hast found, and can not possess those perfections which the certain and necessary conceptions of thy reason have ascribed to him. But if thou hast found him, why is it that thou dost not perceive what thou hast found? Why, O Lord God, does not my soul perceive thee, if it has found thee? Since it has found that which is light and truth has it not found thee? For how could it know this except by seeing the light and the truth! Or could it know anything whatever concerning thee except through thy light and thy truth? If, therefore, it has seen light and truth it has seen thee; if it has not seen thee it has seen neither light nor truth. Is that both light and truth which it has seen, and still has it not as yet seen thee, because it has seen thee only in part, but not as thou art? O Lord, my God, my Creator and Regenerator, say to my longing soul what else thou art than what it has seen, that it may clearly see what it desires. It strives to see more, but beyond what it has already seen, it sees nothing but darkness. Nay, rather, it sees not darkness, for there is no darkness in thee; but it sees itself unable to see more on account of its own darkness. Why this? O Lord, why this? Is its eye darkened by its own weakness, or dazzled by thy splendor? Surely it is both darkened in itself and dazzled by thee. It is also obscured by its own shortness of vision and opprest by thine immensity. It is limited by its own narrow range, and is overpowered by thine amplitude. For how vast is that light from which every truth radiates that dawns upon the rational mind! How capacious is that truth which includes in itself everything that is true, and out of which there exists only nothingness and falsehood! How infinite the mind which sees at a single glance all that has ever occurred; and which knows by whom and through whom and in what way all things have been created from nothing! What purity, what simplicity, what certitude, what glory is here! This surely transcends all that the created mind is able to comprehend.

That the Light Which God Inhabits Is Inaccessible

Truly, O Lord, this is light inaccessible in which thou dwellest; for truly no other being can penetrate this light to contemplate thee there. Truly, therefore, I look not upon it, for it is too resplendent for me; and yet it is through this that I see whatsoever I do see; just as a weak eye sees what it does see, through the light of the sun; while it is unable to gaze upon that light in the sun itself. My intelligence can not approach to thy light, nor comprehend it, so great is its effulgence, nor can the eye of my mind long endure to gaze thereon. It is dazzled by its brightness, overpowered by its amplitude, opprest by its immensity, confounded by its profusion. O, supreme and inaccessible Light! O, per-

fect and blessed Truth! How far thou art
from me, who am so near to thee! How re-
mote from my sight, who am so constantly in
thine! Thou art everywhere present and
entire, yet I see thee not. In thee I move,
and in thee I am, and yet I am unable to
approach unto thee. Thou art within me,
and around me, yet I perceive thee not.

That In God There Is Harmony, Order, Savor, Polish, and Beauty, In a Manner Ineffable and Peculiar to Himself

As yet, O Lord, thou art concealed from my
soul in thine own light and blessedness, and
therefore it yet remains involved in its darkness and misery. For it looks around, but
sees not thy beauty. It hearkens, but hears
not thy harmony. It exercises the sense of
smell, but perceives not thine odor; of taste,
but it recognizes not thy savor; of touch, but
it feels not thy polish. For thou hast in thyself, O Lord, in a manner ineffable and peculiar to thee, all those qualities which thou
hast imparted, under the forms of sense, to
the things which thou hast created; but the
senses of my soul are benumbed, stupefied,
obstructed by the inveterate languor of sin.

That God Alone Is What He Is and Who He Is

Thou alone, O Lord, art what thou art and who thou art. For that which is one thing in its whole and another in its parts, and in which there is anything mutable, is not what it is in an absolute sense. And that which begins from non-existence and can be conceived of as not existing, and which, unless it subsist through something else, must return to non-existence; also whatever has a past which is now no longer, and a future which is yet to come, this does not exist in proper and absolute sense. But thou art what thou art; because whatsoever thou art at any time or in any manner, thou art this at all times and absolutely. And thou art who thou art properly and simply; because thou hast neither a past nor a future, but only a present, neither canst thou be conceived of as not existing at any moment. But thou art life and light and wisdom and blessedness and eternity, and many things good of this nature, and yet thou art none other than the one Supreme Good, absolutely self-sufficient, needing nothing, but whom all things else need in order to their existence and well-being.

That This Supreme Good Is Equally the Father and the Son and the Holy Spirit; That He Is the Only Necessary Being; That He Is the Whole, the Absolute, the Only Good

Thou art this good, O God; the Father; and thy Word, that is thy Son, is this good. For in the Word, by which thou dost declare thyself, there can be nothing else than what thou art, nor anything either greater or less, since thy Word is as true as thou art veracious. And therefore thy Word is, as thou art, Truth itself, and not another truth than thou art; and so simple art thou that nothing else than what thou art can spring from thee. This same good is Love identical with that which is common to thee and to thy Son, that is to say, it is the Holy Spirit proceeding from the Father and the Son. For this same Love is not inferior to thee nor to thy Son; for, so far as thou lovest thyself and the Son, and so far as the Son loves thee and himself, so great art thou and he; this can not be anything different from thyself and thy Son, which is not unequal to thyself and to him; nor can anything proceed from absolute simplicity, but that itself from which it proceeds. But that which

118

each is, this the whole Trinity is, at one and the same time, Father, Son, and Holy Spirit, since each is no other than simple and absolute unity, and supreme, absolute simplicity, which can neither be multiplied nor be now one thing and then another. Moreover, there is but one necessary Being; and he in whom is all good is this one necessary Being; nay, he is himself the whole, the one supreme and the only Good.

An Attempt to Conceive the Nature and Vastness of This Good

Now, O my soul, awake and arouse all thy powers; conceive, so far as thou canst, what and how great is thy good. For if all good things are pleasing, consider attentively how pleasing is that good which contains in itself the sweetness of all other things else that are good, and not such sweetness as we experienced in created things, but such as excels this as far as the Creator is superior to the creature. For if life created is good, how good is life creative? If salvation procured is pleasing, how pleasing is that healing power which has procured all salvation? If that wisdom is lovely which consists in a knowledge of things which are formed, how

119

lovely is the wisdom which has formed all things from nothing? In fine, if things that are pleasing afford great delight, what and how great the delight which he affords by whom these pleasing things themselves have been created?

What and How Great Are the Blessings of Those Who Enjoy This Good

O, who shall enjoy this Good! What will he possess and what will he not possess? Surely he will have all that he desires, and nothing which he desires not. For here will be good for the body and for the mind, such as eye hath not seen nor ear heard, nor the heart of man conceived. Why, therefore, O vain man, dost thou rove through a variety of things in search of pleasures for thy body and for thy mind? Fix thy love upon this one Good which comprehends all other good, and it is sufficient. Direct thy desires to this single good which constitutes every species of good, and it is enough. For what dost thou love, O my body? What dost thou desire, O my soul? There, there alone is found whatsoever thou lovest and whatsoever thou desirest. If beauty delights; "the righteous shall shine as the sun." If velocity, or strength, or corporeal freedom, which nothing can oppose;

"they shall be like the angels of God"; for the body "is sown an animal body and it is raised a spiritual body," not indeed by nature, but by divine power. If a long and vigorous life; there is a healthful eternity, and eternal health; for "the righteous shall live forever"; and "the salvation of the righteous is the Lord." If complete satisfaction; they shall be satisfied "when the glory of God shall appear." If satisfaction more than complete; "they shall be abundantly satisfied from the fatness of thy house." If melody delights thee; there choirs of angels chant without cessation, their harmonious praises to God. If pleasure unmixed and free from all impurity; thou shalt cause them to drink of the river of thy pleasure, O God. If wisdom; there wisdom itself, even the wisdom of God presents itself to the contemplation of the righteous. If friendship; they love God more than themselves, and each other as themselves; and God loves them more than they love themselves; because they love him and themselves and each other through him, and he loves himself and them through himself. If concord; they have all one will, for they have no other than the will of God. If power; the will of the righteous will be as omnipotent as that of God. For as God will be able to do whatever he shall will through himself, so they will be able to do whatsoever they shall will through him; because as their will can differ nothing from his, so his will differ nothing from theirs; and whatsoever he shall will must of necessity come to pass. If honor and riches; God will make his good and faithful servants rulers over many things; nay, he will constitute them his children and they shall be called gods; and where his Son shall be, there shall they be; heirs indeed, of God and joint heirs with Christ. If true security; surely as the righteous will be certain that these good things, or rather that this one good will never, by any means fail them, so they will be certain that they will never of their own accord cast it away, that God who loves them will never deprive them of it against their will, and that there is nothing more powerful than God which can separate them from him against his will and their own. But what and how great is this joy, where such and great good is found? O heart of man, poor and needy heart, inured to trouble and overwhelmed by misery! how wouldst thou rejoice if thou could abound with all this? Ask thy most inward depths if they could contain the joy which would flow from blessedness so great. But surely if any other, whom thou lovest altogether as thyself, should possess the same blessedness, thy joy would be double; for thou wouldst rejoice not less for him than for thyself. But if two, three, or a still greater number should partake of the same, thou wouldst rejoice as much for each one as for thyself, if thou shouldst love each as thyself. Therefore in this perfected love of innumerable happy angels and men, where no one will love each other less than himself, each one will in like manner rejoice for the other as for himself. If, therefore, the heart of man can scarcely contain its own joy, arising from this great good, how will it find room for the aggregate of such joys? And, indeed, since the more any one loves another, the more he will rejoice in his good; and since in this state of perfect felicity each will love God incomparably more than himself, and all others with him, so he will rejoice more beyond conception, in the felicity of God than in that of himself and of all others with him. But if they shall love God with all the heart, with all the mind and all the soul, so that all the heart and all the mind and all the soul would, notwithstanding, be insufficient for the greatness of their love; surely they will so rejoice with all the heart, with all the mind and with all the soul that the whole heart and mind and soul would be insufficient for the fulness of their joy.

Whether This Is the Fulness of Joy Which the Lord Hath Promised

My God and my Lord, my Hope, and the Joy of my heart, say to my soul, if this is the joy concerning which thou hast spoken to us through thy Son, "Ask and ye shall receive, that your joy may be full." For I have found a fulness of joy, and more than a fulness; for after it has filled the entire man, heart, mind, and soul, a fulness of joy beyond all measure will still remain. It is not, therefore, that all this joy will enter into those who rejoice, but all who are to rejoice will enter into this joy. Say, O Lord, say to the inmost heart of thy servant, if this is the joy into which thy servants are to enter, who enter into the joy of their Lord. But surely this joy in which the chosen shall rejoice neither eye hath seen, nor ear heard, nor hath the heart of man conceived. Therefore, O Lord, I have not as yet told, or even conceived, how great will be their joy who are blest of thee. Their joy will, indeed, be in proportion to their love, and their love will be in proportion to their knowledge. To what extent, then, O Lord, will they know thee, and how much will they love thee? Surely eye hath not seen, nor ear heard, nor

hath the heart of man conceived in this life,
the extent to which they will know and love
thee in the life to come O Lord, I beseech
thee, let me enter into the joy of the Lord who
is God, three and one, blessed for ever!
AMEN.

A Prayer of Charles How

My adorable God, I humbly beseech thee to
accept the sacrifice I here, in all humility, desire to make thee, of the remainder of my life;
to be entirely employed, with the utmost
vigor both of my soul and body, in thy service and adoration. Pardon all the sins and
offenses of my past life, and be pleased to bestow upon me a stedfast faith, an ardent love,
an humble and perfect obedience, and a will
capable of no other inclination than what it
shall continually receive from the absolute
guidance of thy divine will; to which I beg
it may be ever perfectly subservient, with all
readiness and cheerfulness. As all my
thoughts and actions are continually before
thee, so I humbly beseech thee that they may
never be unworthy of thy divine presence, for
Jesus Christ's sake. AMEN.

A Prayer of Ludovicus Palamo

O Lord, forasmuch as all my strength is in thee, grant unto me this grace, that I may allow thee to do whatsoever thou wilt; and that my doing may be to lie still in thy hand, that thou mayest do with me that thing only which is most pleasing to thee. Do thou adorn me with holy virtues, giving unto me humbleness of mind, purity of heart, and all those gifts and graces which thou knowest to be needful for me, and whatsoever thou wouldst have to be in me, whether in body or soul; that so I may be able the better to please thee, the more worthily and faithfully to serve thee, and the more perfectly to love thee. I pray, moreover, that thou wouldst give me grace to arrive at that degree of perfection which thou willest me to reach, and grant unto me the aids and dispositions needful for its attainment. AMEN.

SELECTIONS FROM THE

Sermons On the Song of Solomon

AND

The Devout Meditations

BY

SAINT BERNARD OF CLAIRVAUX

BERNARD OF CLAIRVAUX

"If ever there lived on earth a God-fearing and holy monk, it is St. Bernard of Clairvaux," said Luther. Bernard was one of the most prominent personalities of the twelfth century, of the entire middle ages, and of church history in general. He was born at Fontaines, France, 1090; died at Clairvaux, August 20, 1153; was educated at Chatillon; entered the "new monastery" at Citeaux; and in 1115 became abbot of the daughter monastery founded at Clairvaux. With the schism of 1130 Bernard enters into the first rank of the influential men of his time by espousing the cause of Innocent II. against Anacletus II. How great Bernard's influence was at this time may be seen from his successful opposition to Abelard. Bernard is deeply permeated by the feeling of owing everything to the grace of God, that on the working of God rests the beginning and end of the state of salvation, and that we are to trust only in His grace, not in our works and merits. Bernard has always been regarded as a foremost representative of Christian mysticism. His voluminous writings consist of hymns, epistles, sermons, and theological treatises. The best edition of his works is by J. M. Horstius, revised and enlarged by J. Mabillon, Paris, 1667, corrected and enlarged 1690 annd 1719, and reprinted in Migne's "Patrologiæ, Series Latina," vols. clxxxii-clxxxv. An English translation by S. J. Eales of the "Life and Works of St. Bernard of Clairvaux" is in 4 vols., London, 1888-1897.

Bernard of Clairvaux.

Of Wandering Thoughts in Prayer

Have mercy upon me, O God, and assist
me against myself; for such is my infirmity
that there especially do I fall into sin, where
my obligations and endeavors are most indispensable to avoid and reform it. I am
ashamed to think how often I pray, and all
the while regard not what I speak. Thus do
I pray with the mouth, but not with the
spirit; for while my mind is rambling, my
tongue runs over empty forms. My body
indeed is in the closet of the church, but my
heart is at a distance—in the play-house, at
the exchange, in a hundred other places; and
then what wonder, if all I say be lost and
fruitless? For what can it possibly signify
for the voice to perform its part never so
punctually, if the mind in the meanwhile
give no manner of attention? And can there
be any greater perverseness, greater insolence, greater madness, than to turn the deaf
ear and run after trifles and impertinences,
when we take upon us to converse with the
Majesty of heaven and earth in prayer?
Can there on the other hand be anything
more senseless, more provoking than for vile
earth and ashes to behave itself negligently,

and not to think the great Creator of the universe worth listening to, when he vouchsafes to speak to us by his Scriptures and his ministers. But especially, can anything compare with that unwearied patience and forbearance, that mercy and condescension of a gracious and forgiving God, which sees such wretches every day turning the deaf ear, "refusing the voice of the charmer, charm he never so wisely," hardening their hearts and regardless of their own duty and advantage, and yet, instead of taking speedy vengeance, repeats his kind invitations and cries aloud, "O ye simple ones, how long will ye love simplicity, and scorners delight in scorning, and fools hate knowledge?" "Turn ye at my reproof, consider your ways, and be wise. Be still, and commune with your own hearts, and know that I am God."

God speaks to me, and I to him in a psalm; and yet so great is my stupidity that I often repeat the words without ever regarding the subject and the sense, the author, or the design of it. And can I be guilty of a greater disrespect, a more manifest injury to Almighty God, than when I beseech him to hear those prayers which I myself who make them do not attend to, nor know what goes out of my mouth at the very instant of pronouncing? I expect God should have a particular

regard to me, while I have none at all either
to him or to myself: nay, can I hope for
any benefit, while I do which is worse; while
I bring into his presence a heart full of vain,
and loose, impure, and sinful thoughts, and
so offend his sight with corruption and filth,
which is not indeed a heart, but the loathsome,
stinking carcass of a heart.

The Fickleness of Man's Heart

Nothing can be more restless and fleeting,
no part of my nature is so perpetually changing as my heart; every time it gives me the
slip and lets itself loose to unprofitable and
wicked thoughts, it does certainly break off
from God, and transgress its duty to him.
And how exceeding vain and trifling, how
wandering and unsettled is this strolling vaga-
bond; never fixing, while following its own
will, and not steering by the guidance and
counsel of God? For itself is a perpetual
motion, without any principle of rest from
within; and therefore it outstrips the swift-
est bodies, is under a thousand different de-
terminations at once, and flies about in quest
of objects innumerable. It makes experi-
ments, but to no purpose; seeks rest everywhere, but finds it nowhere; is sure of labor
and disappointment, and all the misery these

can bring, but happiness flies from it, and its pursuits have never their hoped-for end. It is not so much as consistent with itself, but disagrees and flies off from its own proposals; changes its inclinations and aversions, loves and hates, dislikes old, and takes new measures: starts fresh projects, sets up and pulls down, and runs the race over and over again; turns things this way, and that way, and every way; and all this from its own mercurial nature, that can lie still nowhere, but must be always in action, tho it act in contradiction to itself. This is what I have often represented to myself by a windmill, which whirls about apace, and takes all you put into it, grinds all you pour; but if you pour in nothing, still it goes; and, for want of other materials to employ it, sets itself on fire. Just thus my heart is always at work, asleep or awake it stands not; but either by dreams, or by such waking thoughts as oftentimes are very little better, it is still under sail, and nothing comes amiss to it. Again, as sand and stones if put into the mill break it, pitch or dirt foul it, chaff chokes it up; so is it with this heart of mine. Afflicting thoughts disturb it, unclean pollute it, idle and unprofitable ones tire and harass it. And thus it will be, while it neglects spiritual and future good, and does not observe the law

of God for its rule, and attain his assistance
for its support; all its confusion grows in
proportion as it is more estranged from the
love of heavenly things and entangled with
the bewitching but always empty and treacherous objects here below.

Now when the soul falls from those worthy,
and is bewildered in these sordid affections,
vanity seizes it, curiosity distracts it, covetous
desires allure it, pleasure seduces it, luxury
defiles it, envy racks it, anger ruffles it, grief
afflicts and depresses it; and thus, obnoxious
to every kind of misery, it is overwhelmed
and sunk in all manner of vice; and all because it forsook God, which singly was the
good large enough to answer all its wants
and wishes. The mind is dissipated and scattered among a multitude of trifles; and, tho
it anxiously seek for satisfaction, can yet attain to none till it return to that one all-
sufficient object. It roves from thought to
thought, tumbles about like a feverish man,
and tries to find that ease from variety which
the quality and intrinsic value of the things
themselves are not able to furnish. Thus
miserably does the heart of man fall, till it
become even misery in the abstract; for such
it is, when abandoned to its own folly and
deprived of the direction and assistance of
divine grace. But when it returns and re-

tires into itself, and comes nicely to examine what are the fruits of all its past solicitude, it finds itself deluded and nothing remaining in hand, because the whole result of all this care is no real substance, but only an anxious thought, a fantastical airy notion, that compounds an imaginary being out of wild ideals of its own forming: and thus men are deceived by an empty phantom, which the devil and his temptations industriously drest up, that its false beauties might be qualified effectually to cheat them into ruin. My God commands me to give him my heart, and my disobedience to his command renders me at the same time a rebel to my own best reason. For the conditions of my duty are so ordered that I can not live in subjection to myself, but by living in subjection to him; and all I do in compliance with my own mind comes hard and strained and goes against the grain, because I have not got the mastery of my own heart so as to serve God willingly and cheerfully. The neglecting to fix my heart upon its proper business is the occasion of its laying more plots in one single minute than all mankind are able to accomplish in multitudes of years. So long as I am not united with God, I am divided in and at perpetual strife with myself. Now this union with God can be secured only by char-

ity, this subjection to him must be grounded
in humility, and that humility again must
be the result of my knowing and believing
the truth and having right notions of God
and myself.

Highly necessary, therefore, and of great
use it is that I inquired diligently, and discover the true state of my soul, that I be
duly sensible how vile, how frail, how liable
to change, and corruption I am. Then, having found the extreme sinfulness and misery
of my nature, my next care must be to lay
hold upon and hold fast by him, from whom
I derive my being, without whom I neither
am anything nor able to do anything. And
because it is by sin I have departed from my
God, the way to come back to him again must
needs be by true confession and repentance
of those sins, which have set me at so wide a
distance from him. In the confession of our
faults, we should proceed with all possible
sincerity and diligence, and act without any
private reserves—a thing too seldom done;
for how few are there, who, when they declare the facts committed, lay open all the
circumstances, all the wicked means and ends
by which their guilt was aggravated? Nay,
how unusual is it punctually to confess the
very facts, some of which time and negligence
have worn out all impression of, or if not so,

yet when we look back, the number appears so
great that we content ourselves with general
terms, and think it endless to descend to par-
ticulars. Again, in our confessions, how little are we touched with an abhorrence of that
turpitude and baseness, which ought to be
the most powerful, but is commonly the weak-
est motive to that shame and remorse we feel
upon the account of our sins? If we call
in the advice of our guides, and open our
case to a spiritual physician, how do we man-
gle and disguise our confessions, revealing
one part to one, another to another, relating
things imperfectly, showing them in false
lights, and contriving not so much to inform
as to keep them in ignorance what sort of
persons we really have been? This is the
reason that so little benefit is received from
their ghostly counsels and comforts, because
we dissemble the matter; and when they speak
peace, our own conscience can upbraid us
with hypocrisy, and tell us that those absolu-
tions do not of right belong to us which we
have obtained purely by our own fraudulent
management, while concealing the blackest
and most dangerous part of our crimes. For
we are not to suppose that any confession
will do us service, except it be attended with
truth and simplicity of heart; nor will the
release given by God's ministers upon earth

avail the sinner for pardon any farther than as the case represented to those servants and officers agrees with that state of it which lies before their all-seeing Master in heaven.

But to all this perhaps may be objected, what need of any application at all to these spiritual guides, or why should our offenses be told to any man, since God alone can pardon them, and what men do will stand us in no stead, till it be ratified in the court above? To all this, take not mine, but the apostle's answer, "Confess your sins to one another, and pray one for another." Some offenses are not only against God, but against our brethren too, and ought to be acknowledged to the injured party, in order to satisfaction and reconciliation. Others may be imparted profitably; either for advice in doubtful and difficult cases, where partiality or want of skill may incapacitate us for making a right judgment of our distemper or its proper remedies, or else to engage the assistance and intercession of our friends; on all which and some other accounts it may be very convenient, if not absolutely necessary, to disclose our sins to God's priests, who are qualified to be faithful and wise counsellors, fervent and powerful intercessors for us. And well it were if men, who have been proudly and obstinately rebellious against God, would exercise this discipline upon themselves, and undergo the humiliation of acknowledging their own vileness to his ministers. Well, if they would take this method of having their condition and their concern for it particularly recommended in the affectionate prayers of those whom their function obliges to be the most tender lovers of souls, this might have excellent effects, both in increasing their own compunction and in disposing God to pity it; and as this taking of shame upon ourselves might facilitate the cure of what is past, so would it doubtless be a mighty check to men, where secrecy is a prevailing temptation, and render them more circumspect for the time to come. This is what all serious and considerate persons must allow to be highly expedient, tho it be not indispensably necessary: for where the heart is duly humbled, the sin sufficiently lamented, the man effectually reformed, we have no reason to believe that God will not accept the performance of that work upon confession to himself alone; in which our confessing to men can be no further serviceable than that it is a probable means of having it performed more effectually than (ordinarily speaking) it was like to have been without such confession.

Of Excusing Our Faults

How often, when I have set myself to make an entire confession of my faults, have I added to their number and guilt, instead of purging and amending them? How often, when any of them were charged upon me, have I either falsely disowned them, or cunningly shifted them off, or softened and disguised them, by artificial colors and plausible extenuations? Nay, which is worse than all these, how often have I abandoned all modesty and shame, and impudently defended what I ought to have blushed for, and been enraged beyond all patience to be charged with those things which my own conscience told me all the while were very just accusations? And indeed what accusations are not just? For there is no sort of wickedness but I either actually have been or, had I been left to my own corrupt inclinations, should most certainly have been polluted with it. And therefore it is fit that in a due sense of my abominations, and an humble reflection upon all the rest which I was naturally disposed to, I should lay my hand upon my mouth, bewail my grievous transgressions, and the misery and wrath they have most justly exposed me to; seriously intend and promise a thorough reformation; take sanctuary in no trifling pretenses or extenuating shifts; submit to think as ill of myself as I deserve, and patiently take the reproofs and admonitions of others; in a word, so demean myself with regard to past faults that they may not rise up any more against me, and for the future avoid offending with all possible diligence. For if I thus judge and condemn myself, I shall not be condemned of the Lord.

A Further Confession of Sins

My transgressions have contributed to the destruction not of myself alone, but of many besides: for, being conscious to myself how heinous and numerous my own crimes have been, I feel a secret shame and fear which restrains me from reproving others when they do amiss. And thus I become accessory to the death of their souls too by tamely suffering that poison to spread, the malignity whereof might be expelled by timely warning or sharp reprehensions. I take it ill of them who rebuke me for my faults, and hate them whom this friendly office should have taught me to prefer before those false pretenders to friendship, whose treacherous complaisance chooses to see me eternally undone, rather than to save me from hell, by this most profitable but distasteful piece of service. When anything created me uneasiness, my impatience hath tempted me to wish that it might cease to be, or that it never had been at all; and yet upon recollection, I could not but acknowledge that he who made everything is good, and that everything he made is very good in its own nature; and consequently, if it proved evil to me in the event, or the effects of it, the only reason must be that I myself was evil, and lacked the grace and prudence to make a right use of it. For after all, nothing can work me mischief except myself. The harm that I sustain I carry about with me, and never am a real sufferer but by own fault. I have been so extravagant as to wish that God might want either the will or power to take vengeance on my sins; which what is it in truth but to desire that he were defective in his most essential excellence, his wisdom and knowledge, his justice and omnipotence? And yet supposing him to be so, he must at the same time cease to be God. No pride was more excessive than mine, which above all other vices renders salvation hazardous. For God always looks upon this disposition with a very jealous eye; he can not away with it, nor be reconciled to it. He dwells with the contrite and humble; but the same indignation on which would not endure pride in the same heaven with himself makes him disdain to dwell by his grace in the same breast with it. It is true, this vice was born and first appeared in heaven; but, as if by some strange infatuation it had forgot the way by which it fell thence, it never could get up thither again. When the weather is foul, or extremely cold or hot, I have been so wicked and unreasonable as to repine and murmur against Providence. So dexterous are we grown in wickedness, as to turn those things into occasions and improvements of our sins which the bounty of that Providence sends us for the conveniences of life. And since we thus contrive to make everything contribute to our wickedness, it is but just in God so to order the matter that nothing should be incapable of becoming instrumental to our punishment. In the performance of my public devotions, I have often put my voice to the stretch, and been more solicitous for a pathetical delivery or a musical cadence than for the fervency and inward zeal of my heart. But God, who is privy to the most secret thoughts, is not to be imposed upon by shows and sounds; he looks not at the agreeableness of the voice, but at the purity and pious disposition of the soul. And too often it happens that he who charms the people with the sweetness of his tones does but grate the ears of God and provoke him by the perverseness of his temper and behavior.

How often hath my importunity extorted from my friends or spiritual guides leave to indulge myself in some particular liberty which they thought inconvenient? Not considering (fool that I am) that he does not deceive himself who takes pains to work his advisers up to a compliance with his own inclinations, in opposition to their own impartial and better sense. I have allowed myself in coveting or indirectly procuring things of small value, and flattered my conscience with an idle fancy that the sin was not worth repenting of, because the price of what I got was inconsiderable: and yet the reason of the thing convinces me that the obliquity of any action is to be measured, not by the value of the advantage I propose from it, but by the depravity of the corrupt affection which pursues that advantage inordinately. For he that is unfaithful in little will also be unfaithful in much; and it is not the object, but the desire and the undue methods of obtaining it, that constitutes the essence of the sin. When I was employed in business, I have not taken all the pains I might or ought to have done. When I enjoyed leisure and retirement, I have been perfectly thoughtless, and this is certainly a great offense, to neglect the improvement of such happy opportunities. For no man ought so to sequester himself from the world as not to make his solitude turn to some good account for the benefit of others; nor should any be so deeply engaged in the business of the world as not to leave room for God and heavenly contemplations. And he is but a very indifferent proficient who does not always consult and promote the good of others, when it lies in his power. I have been often guilty of that worst and most wicked of all vanities, the boasting of my sins; fondly imagining that to be my glory which was in truth my shame and fault. Nay so perversely have I managed, as even to turn my virtues into vices. For justice, when it exceeds on the rigorous side, degenerates into cruelty; and excess of piety and good nature encourages offenders by too great an easiness, and by relaxation of that discipline which should constrain them to better manners: and thus it often happens, that what men value as an excellence is really vice and great defect. Thus sloth and a tame insensibility passes for a quiet spirit and meekness of disposition. I have pretended to be what I was not, profest to desire what I secretly hated or feared, and to dread and refuse what I passionately desired: my tongue and my heart were often very distant, and I have acted the fox under sheep's clothing. For what are the qualities of a dissembling fox, if these that follow be not?—A lukewarm behavior, a sensual mind, counterfeit confessions of sin, fits of remorse that last but a little while and return but very seldom, obedience without cheerfulness, prayer without devotion, reading without edification, talk without mature consideration?

O how harsh and cutting are any reflections of this kind to me, because I am conscious that all the edge of them is turned upon my own soul? But tho this be my wretched case, yet, if I do not disown or cover my faults, but with all humility and sorrow confess myself a most vile, miserable sinner, some hope there is that with my righteous and merciful Judge the acknowledgment of my offenses may prevail for a pardon. I will therefore pour out my complaint before him, and declare the worst of my condition, that so, if it be possible, his bowels may relent and yearn over one lost, unworthy of compassion, upon any other account than only as extremity of misery can recommend me to it. There shall not a sin be left uninquired after, or concealed when found; for the first step toward heaven is to see and lament the near approaches we have made to hell. I have gone on in great security, as if those outward appearances of religion which the station I

am in obliges me to would do the business.
But alas! these are a deceitful trial; and outside may look fair and promise well; but wo
to him who trusts to that without attending
to the rottenness within and the worm that
gnaws at his heartstrings. To such circumstances we may apply that of Hosea: "Strangers have devoured his strength, and he knoweth not, yet, gray hairs are here and there
upon him, yet he knoweth it not." Thus I,
like Ephraim heretofore, fixing my thoughts
and care wholly upon the things that are
without, and ignorant and unconcerned how
matters stand within, am poured out like
water, and become altogether unprofitable and
vain. The past I forget, the present I dis-
regard, and the future I make no provision
for. The mercies and benefits I receive I am
unthankful for, the temptations to evil I feel
a wondrous forwardness to comply with; but
the motions and persuasions to anything that
is good make slight impressions, and find me
slow and heavy.

Self=Examination

This duty of self-examination, which I am now upon, I find at once a plain necessity for, and yet a mighty discouragement from. For, if I do not nicely look into my soul, I shall continue ignorant of my own condition; and if I do, the ghastliness and deformity that I discover there make me a perfect monster and a terror to myself. The matter for reproof and confusion which appears there is wofully great; and yet the oftener and more narrowly I set about this search, the more lurking abominations still I bring to light. How should it indeed be otherwise, since every corner of my heart is a cage of unclean birds; since every day from my first beginning to sin hath made additions to the black account; and even now, tho sensible of my wretchedness, I do not cease to heap new guilt upon the former? The offenses which are plainly before my eyes I can look upon without any sensible concern; I see that which ought to make me ashamed exceedingly, yet am not the least out of countenance at it; and that which should even break my heart with grief gives me no manner of uneasiness. But this is surely a mortal symptom, and a sad indication of a damnable state. For do we not conclude that member dead which feels no pain? Do we not know by long experience that the patient is then incurable when grown insensible of his disease? And yet, wretch that I am, this is my case. I am thoughtless and dissolute, airy and wanton, and do not take any care to correct my extravagancies or to fix my wandering mind. I confess my sins every day, and yet repeat them, and am not made so wise, either by my own danger and disasters, or those of other men, as to avoid the pit into which I have fallen myself, or seen my brethren fall, or perhaps, indeed, have thrust them into. Prayers and tears are the best refuge I can take, and subjects in abundance I have ministered for them, by the many evil things I have done and the good I have neglected to do. But alas! I find myself not at all touched as these occasions require. Quite contrary, my devotion is but lukewarmness at the best. Nay, I languish, I grow cold, and pray without any manner of warmth; and as to remorse for my sins, my soul is perfectly benumbed and senseless. I know upon recollection that I am in a miserable state, and yet can not shed one tear for my misery; because I have long continued to harden my heart, God hath now made my fault my punishment, and withdrawn the grace of tender tears and godly sorrow from me.

Conscience Is Everywhere

It is the fondest imagination in the world to suppose that I can either commit sin unobserved or conceal it after commission; for let the privacy I effect be never so close, still it is not possible to shut out, or run away from, my own conscience. This will be sure to bear me company, and it always carries about with it all I have ever laid up there, whether it be good or whether it be evil. There is no trustee to be compared with this for fidelity and punctual dealing. Whatever is deposited in its custody is in safe hands, it keeps it for the man as long as he lives, and will be sure to pay down in full tale at the day of death. If I do amiss, this is present with me; if I do well and feel a satisfaction in it, that resentment proves that conscience is with me and marks my behavior. It never parts with me in this world, and it will follow me into the next; and wheresoever I am, according to the quality of what I trust it with, it never fails to reproach and shame or else to commend and exalt me. Thus there is not only an evidence of a judgment, but even the thing itself, in the breast of every one of us. We have no need to look abroad for justice, since God hath erected

a tribunal at home, and so ordered the matter
that those of a man's own household should
go through the whole process upon him; for
here are informers and witnesses, judges and
executioners. When I break the law, my
conscience accuses me, my memory testifies
against me, my reason tries and judges me;
sensual pleasure is my prison, fear my exe-
cutioner, and sinful delectation my penalty.
For in proportion to the delights which ac-
companied the sin, the torments are multiplied and heightened in the punishment. And
God is just and wise in ordaining that our
very sins should prove our punishments, and
that the pleasures of sin and the pains we
feel for them should both spring out of the
same root.

Of Three Ways of Contemplating God, Represented Under the Figure of Three Storerooms

[The King hath brought me unto his storerooms.—
Song of Songs 1 : 3, Douay.]

Lo, here is the source of fragrance; here
is the point toward which we run. The Bride
had said that we must press forward, and in
what strength; but whither our course was
to be directed, she had not said. Now, then,
she declares that it is toward the Lord's store-

rooms, and in the strength of the fragrance
which is exhaled from them. This she press-
es with her characteristic eagerness, and desires to be introduced into his fulness. But,
in the first place, what is to be understood by
these storehouses? Let us, to begin with, imagine that in the dwelling of the Bridegroom
there are chambers fragrant with perfumes
and filled with all kinds of delights. It is in
these that, as in a treasury, is stored and kept
in reserve whatever is most rare and valuable of the products of garden and of field.
Hither, then, do all those who run direct their
steps; but who are they that run? These are
the souls who are fervent in spirit, the Bride,
the maidens in her train; but she whose love
is most ardent runs more swiftly, and arrives
sooner. When she arrives, she suffers no repulse, and not even any delay. Forthwith
the portals are opened to her, as to an inmate
of the house, as to one greatly beloved, who
is especially dear and welcome. But what
as to her maidens? They follow afar off;
they are still weak; they can not press forward with devotion equal to that of the
Bride; they can not experience fervor and
earnest desire such as hers; therefore they arrive later and they remain without. But the
charity of the Bride does not rest, nor does
she pride herself, as is frequently the case,

upon her happy successes so as to be forgetful of them. On the contrary, she consoles them the more assiduously, and exhorts them to endure patiently and calmly the repulse they have received and her absence. Then she declares to them the joy which she has attained, and that for the very reason that they may rejoice with her, in the hope of one day attaining to a share in the graces and blessings of their mother. For she does not so pursue her own advantage as to neglect the care of them, nor desires that her benefit should be hurtful or prejudicial to them. However far removed from them she is by superior merits, it is of necessity that her charity and tender care for them keep her with them always. It is her duty moreover, to follow the example of her Bridegroom, both, on the one hand, in seeking the heavens, and, on the other, in promising to be ever upon the earth with his people, even to the consummation of all things. So also the bride, whatever progress she may make, and whatever advancement she may attain, is prevented by her care, her deep interest and affection for those whom she has begotten in the gospel, from ever leaving them or forgetting them in the depths of her heart.

Let her say then to them: Take courage and rejoice. The King has brought me into his storerooms; regard yourselves as having been thereby brought in also. I alone seem to have entered in, but the advantage is not to me alone. Every advancement of mine is virtually yours; it is for you that I make profit; and I share with you the graces which more than you I have deserved. Do you wish for an unquestionable proof that her words are to be taken in this sense and intention? Then listen to the reply which they make: "We will be glad and rejoice in thee; we do not deserve to do so in ourselves, but in thee." And they add: "We are mindful of thy bosom" (Song of Songs, 1:4); that is, "We shall endure patiently until thou come, knowing that thou wilt return to us with thy bosom filled with graces." We confidently hope then, to rejoice and be glad; meanwhile we are mindful of thee. The words which he adds, "more than wine," signify that they are still touched with the remembrance of the desires of the flesh, which are spoken of as wine, and that, nevertheless, those desires are overcome by the thought of that abounding sweetness, which as they have experienced, flows from her. Now you see what confidence they have with regard to their mother, how they look upon all her advantages and all her joys as belonging to themselves, and console themselves for their own repulse by her admission. They would not have so great confidence, if they did not recognize her as their mother. Let prelates, who like better to make themselves feared by those committed to their charge, than to be useful to them, take this to heart. Be ye learned, O ye that are judges of the earth. Learn from this that you ought to be as mothers, not masters, to your subjects; study to make yourselves loved rather than feared; and if there be need sometimes of severity, let it be that of a father, not of a tyrant. Show yourselves mothers in affection, fathers in reproof. Be gentle, not harsh; be not forward to inflict stripes; let the view of the maternal bosom promise indulgence; let the hearts (of those under you) grow fat with milk, not swell with anger. Why do you lay your heavy yoke upon those whose burden it is rather your duty to bear? Why does the young son who has been bitten by a serpent avoid displaying his wound to the priest, to whom he ought rather to resort as to the bosom of a mother? If ye are spiritual, restore such an one in the spirit of meekness; considering thyself, lest thou also be tempted (Gal. 6:1). For otherwise "he shall die in his sin....but his blood will I require at thine hand" (Ezek. 3:20).

Now, since the context is clear by what I have said above, let us see what is the mysti-

cal meaning of "the storehouse." Later on
mention is made of the garden and also of the
chamber, and I take these three for the subject of our present discussion; for when treated together, they throw light mutually upon
each other. Let us seek them if you please,
these three words in the Holy Scriptures;
the storehouse, the garden, and the chamber.
For a soul that is athirst for God willingly
occupies itself with and lingers in these, knowing that in them it will assuredly find him
whom it thirsts for. Let, then, the garden
represent the plain and simple historical sense
of the Scripture; the storehouse the moral
sense of it; and the chamber the secret and
mystical truth reached by divine contemplation.

In the first place, I think that the historic
sense is not unfitly referred to the garden,
because in the history are found men of many
virtues, as it were fruitful trees in the garden of the Bridegroom and in the paradise of
God; and from their conduct and their actions you may take examples, as from a tree
you gather fruit. Who can question that a
good man is, as it were, a plant of God? Hear
what holy David sings concerning a good
man: "He shall be like a tree planted by the
rivers of water, that bringeth forth his fruit
in his season; his leaf also shall not wither"

(Ps. 1:3). Jeremiah also expresses himself
to the same effect, and in almost the same
words: "He shall be as a tree planted by the
waters, and that spreadeth out her roots by
the river, and shall not see when heat cometh;
but her leaf shall be green" (Jer. 17:8).
And the psalmist: "The righteous shall flour-
ish like the palm-tree; he shall grow like a
cedar in Lebanon" (Ps. 92:12). And of
himself he says: "I am like a green olive-tree
in the house of God" (Ps. 52:8). History
is, then, as it were, a garden, and it is threefold; for it contains the creation, the reconciliation, and the reparation of heaven and
earth. Creation, that is like the sowing or
planting of a garden. Reconciliation is, as
it were, the germination of that which is sown
or planted. For at the due time the heavens
have distilled dew from above, the clouds have
poured down righteousness, the earth has
opened and brought forth the Savior (Isa.
45:8), by whom was brought about the reconciliation of heaven and earth. For he is
our peace who hath made both one (Eph.
2:14), reconciling by his blood all things,
whether in earth or heaven (Col. 1:20).
Reparation, again, is to come to pass at the
ending of the dispensation. For there shall
be a new heaven and a new earth; the good
shall be gathered from among the evil, to be

set in safety in the storehouse of God, as
fruits from a garden. In that day, it is
said, shall the branch of the Lord be beautiful and glorious, and the fruit of the earth
shall be excellent and comely (Isa. 4:2). In
this garden of the historic sense then, you
have three periods included.

In the moral sense, secondly, you have a
threefold discipline: three cells, as it were,
in one storehouse. Therefore it is, perhaps,
that they are spoken of in the plural as
"storerooms," in contemplation of this number of cells. A little further on, the Bride
felicitates herself on having been brought
into the "cellar of wine" (2:4, "banqueting
house," A. V.). We, then, because we read,
"Give an occasion to a wise man and he will
be wiser" (Prov. 9:9), take occasion from
this name, which the Holy Spirit has thought
fit to give to this cell, to give it also to the
two others; to call one the cell of perfumes,
the other that of unguents. We shall explain
presently the reason for these names. But
in the meantime notice that all which sur-
rounds the Bridegroom is sweet, as all is
salutary—wine, perfumes, and unguents.
Wine, the Scripture declares, maketh glad
the heart of man (Ps. 104:15). We read also
that oil maketh the face cheerful, and it is
with oil and medicinal powders that oint-

ments or unguents are compounded. Lastly,
perfumes are not only agreeable by their odor,
but are useful because of their medicinal virtue. It is, then, with good reason that the
Bride rejoices at having been brought into a
spot where graces are so great and so abundant.

But I have other names also for them, for
which, as I consider, a still greater probabil-
ity may be shown. To name them in their
order, I take the first cell to be that of discipline, the second that of nature, the last that
of grace. In the first you learn, following
the rule of Christian ethics, to be the last
of all; but in the second to be equal to all,
and in the last to be superior to all; that is
to say, you learn how to act as an inferior,
how to act as an equal, and how to act as a
superior; or, again, to be below, to be beside,
to be above others. In the first you learn to
be a disciple, in the second to be a companion,
in the third to be a master. Nature has, indeed, made all men equal; but that natural
order having been corrupted by pride, men
have become impatient of that equality, desirous to elevate themselves above others, and
full of efforts to do so; greedy of vainglory,
envying and provoking one another. Thus,
first of all, insolence of character requires to
be restrained by the yoke of discipline, until

the stubborn will, worn down by observance of the severe and constantly repeated rules of the elders, may be humbled and cured, and regain by its obedience that good of nature which it had lost by the indulgence of pride, until the man shall have learned to possess his soul in patience, and to live peacefully and kindly, as far as in him lies, with his fellow creatures; that is to say, with all men; and that not by fear of punishment, but by the spontaneous impulse of the will. Then he will pass on into the cell of nature, and will make proof of that which is written: "Behold how good and how pleasant it is for brethren to dwell together in unity. It is like the precious ointment upon the head" (Ps. 133:1, 2). For characters thus disciplined are, as it were, sweet spices pounded together, from which is composed the oil of joy, which is the good of nature, and a sweet and excellent unguent is produced from it. The man who is, so to speak, anointed with this becomes peaceful and amiable; one who provokes no quarrel, who deceives no one, who attacks no one, who offends no one; who does not set himself above others, or prefer himself to any one else, but, on the contrary, maintains with those around him a continual interchange of kindnesses given and received.

I think that if you have clearly understood

the leading characteristics of the two former cells, you will be of the opinion that I have not unfitly named the one that of perfumes, the other that of unguents. For in the former, as the forcible pounding of a pestle forces and extracts the strength and fragrance of spices, so the pressure of the rule and the rigor of discipline expresses, so to speak, and draws forth the natural force of the characters of those who are ruled. And in the latter the agreeable sweetness of a voluntary and, so to speak, innate affection runs eagerly of its own accord, like, as it were, the fragrant oil which is upon the head, and which at the slightest touch of warmth rolls downward and is diffused over the whole body. Thus in the cell of discipline are enclosed, as it were, the simple materials of perfumes in a dry state, and thus I have thought it ought to be called "of perfume." But in that which is said to be of nature, the unguents compounded of these are found and are stored, and therefore it is called "of unguents." As for the wine-cellar, I suppose that the reason for the name is no other than that in it is stored the wine of a zeal fervent with charity. One who has not as yet deserved to be brought into this cell should assuredly not be set in authority over others. For it is essential that one who has

the direction of others should be fervent
with this wine, in like manner as was the
great Doctor of the Gentiles, when he said,
"Who is weak, and I am not weak? Who is
offended, and I burn not?" (2 Cor. 11:29).
Otherwise, it is altogether wrong that you
should aspire to rule over those to whom you
have no desire to be of service, and should
claim for yourself, with excessive ambition,
the subjection of those whose salvation you
are not earnestly desirous to forward. This
cell I have named that of grace, not because
it is possible to obtain even the two others
without grace, but because of the fulness
of grace which is reached in this alone. For
"love is the fulfilling of the law," and "he
that loveth another hath fulfilled the law"
(Rom. 13:10, 8).

You have seen the reason of the names;
see now the different characters of the cells;
for it is one thing to repress by fear, and by
the rigid rule of discipline, the wanton and
wandering senses and the irregular appetites of the flesh, and another to preserve
a kindly agreement with brethren by a spontaneous disposition to do so. These differ in
difficulty and, indeed, in the faculties which
effect them; and so also to live a regulated
life under the authority of another, and to
do so with our own will for the only con-

straining influence, are altogether distinct
things. In the same way, no one will declare
the living in peace and on good terms with
others and the ruling over them for their
benefit to be actions of equal merit and re-
quiring the same powers. How many are
there who live in peace under the direction
of an intelligent guide, whom, if they were set
free from the obligation to obey, they would
speedily perceive not to be able to remain
even peaceful and harmless to their neighbors? And similarly there are very many
who are seen to conduct themselves simply
and without offense among their brethren
who, if they were set over them, would behave themselves so as to be not only useless,
but even unwise and harmful. Such persons
ought to content themselves within the bounds
of a mediocrity which is advantageous to
them, following the measure of the grace
which God has bestowed upon them; not having, indeed, any great need of a master, but
yet being unfitted to be masters themselves.
These, indeed, are of a more excellent character than the former class; but such as know
how to govern well are superior both to the
one and to the other. Those, too, who are
faithful and wise in ruling over the Lord's
household have it in promise from him that
he will make them rulers over all his goods

(Matt. 24:48). But as there are few who
rule wholly to the advantage of others, so
there are fewer still who do so with humility.
Yet both the one and the other duty are
easily fulfilled by him who has attained perfect discretion, the mother of all the virtues,
and has drunk of the wine of charity to the
point of contemning his own glory, and of
entire forgetfulness of himself, so that he
seeketh not his own; and this state is reached
only in the cell called "of wine," and under
the wonderful guidance of the Holy Spirit.
The virtue of discretion lies prone and helpless without the fervor of charity, while
the vehement fervor of charity without
the moderating influence of discretion hur-
ries onto the precipice. Therefore he is
to be praised to whom neither is wanting, insomuch that fervor animates his discretion, and discretion regulates his fervor.
So it behooves him to be constituted who rules
over others. But I should regard him as the
highest in character, and as having learned
perfectly the sum of this discipline, upon
whom has been bestowed the power to pass
through and around all these cellars without
stumbling; who in no respect whatever either
resists his superiors, envies his equals, or toward his inferiors commits either the error
of being wanting in care for them, or ruling

them in pride; who is obedient to those who
are above him, to his companions obliging,
to those under him kindly condescending for
their good; which high degree of perfection,
indeed, I have no hesitation in attributing to
the Bride. This is intimated in the state-
ment she has made, that "The King hath
brought me into his storehouses," since she
mentions not some one only, but speaks in
the plural, "his storehouses."

Now let us pass to the bedchamber. What
is that chamber? Have I the presumption to
think that I know what it is? By no means
do I arrogate to myself any experience of so
exalted a subject, nor do I boast of a preroga-
tive, which is reserved to the happy Bride
alone, being careful, according to that prov-
erb of the Greeks, to "know myself," and to
know, as did the psalmist (in a similar case)
that "such knowledge is too wonderful for
me; it is high, I can not attain unto it" (Ps.
139: 6). If I had no knowledge whatever, I
should say nothing. What little I do know
I will not enviously keep back from you;
what I do not know, may he, "who teacheth
man knowledge" (Ps. 94: 10), vouchsafe to
impart to you. I have already said, and I
dare say that you remember, that the chamber of the King is to be sought in the secret
and mystical truth reached by divine con-

templation. But, as in speaking of perfumes, I said that the Bridegroom has many, and of different kinds, and that all of these are not bestowed upon everyone, but that each has part in them, according to the various character of his discernings, so I think of the chamber of the King also, that it is not one, but many. Nor has he one queen also, but assuredly very many; he has many woman friends, and of maidens the number is uncounted. Each of these has her secret confidence with the Bridegroom, and says: "My secret is for myself, my secret is for myself" (Isa. 24:16). It is not granted to all to enjoy in the same degree the dear and secret presence of the Bridegroom, but it is given to whomsoever it has been prepared by the Father. For we have not chosen him, but he has chosen us, and established us in our place; and wheresoever any soul has been placed by him, there is he with that soul. One woman, moved with penitence, found her place at the feet of the Lord Jesus (Luke 7:38); another, if it were really another, found the fruit of her devotion at the head of Jesus (Matt. 26:7). St. Thomas attained the grace of that secret (favor) at his side, St. John leaning upon his breast, St. Peter in the bosom of the Father, and St. Paul in the third heaven.

Who of us can worthily distinguish between these varieties of merits, or rather of rewards? Nevertheless, that I may not seem to pass over in silence that which is within our knowledge, notice that the former of the women mentioned sought her safety under the shelter of humility; the latter in the seat of hope; St. Thomas in firmness of faith; St. John in breadth of charity; St. Paul in the depth of wisdom; St. Peter in the light of truth. If then, in the (home of the) Bridegroom there are many mansions, each, whether queen or friend, and even she who is only of the number of the maidens, finds place and lodgment there proportioned to her merits, and is permitted to remain there until she passes beyond it by inspiring contemplation, enters into the joy of her Lord, and of the sweet secrets of the Bridegroom explores the utmost depths. . . . Now it is sufficient to know that to none, whether of the maidens, or of the friends, or even of the queens, is access opened to that secret of the inner chamber of the Bridegroom, which he reserves for her who is his dove, his undefiled, his only and perfect one. On that account I am not troubled or surprised if access to it is not given unto me, especially because it is to my mind quite clear that not even the Bride attains to the knowledge of all the secret things into which she desires to be admitted. For does she not earnestly ask the Bridegroom where he feeds his flock, and where he rests at noon (Song of Songs 1:6)?

But let me tell you to what point I have arrived, or rather that I think I have reached; for you will not impute vanity to that which I say in the hope of serving you. There is, then, in the dwelling of the Bridegroom a chosen spot in which the Sovereign Ruler of the universe decrees his laws and shapes his designs, setting laws in weight, and measure, and number, to all things created. That place is lofty and secret, but it is by no means noiseless. For tho he, as far as regards himself, disposes all things with sweetness, yet he disposes them, and does not permit that one who has reached that point by contemplation should remain in quiescence; but he wearies, and by a course marvelous and yet delightful, renders full of unrest and lassitude the soul that searches out and admires these deep things. The Bride expresses beautifully, in a latter part of this Canticle, each of these feelings, that is, the delight and, at the same time, the inquietude of this contemplation, as where she says: "I sleep but my heart waketh" (5:2). For in speaking of sleep she signifies that she tastes the repose of a trance most sweet, and the stillness of

complete admiration; but when of waking,
that she endures the weariness of a restless
curiosity and laborious research. Thus the
holy Job says "When I lie down I say, When
shall I arise and the night be gone?" (Job
7:4). Do you not understand by these
words that a holy soul desires to escape from
a repose which, in a certain sense, troubles
it, and to seek again the same employment,
troublous, and yet sweet? For he would not
have said "When shall I arise?" if that repose of contemplation had been entirely pleasing to him; nor, on the other hand, if it had
been wholly displeasing, would he have
awaited with impatience the hour of repose,
that is to say, the evening. That, therefore,
where entire rest is not attained, is not the
bedchamber of the Bridegroom.

There is still another place, in which the
vengeance, most severe and most secret, of
God the Judge, just and terrible in his deal-
ings with the children of men, watches cease-
lessly over his creatures, gifted with reason
but doomed on account of sin. The awe-
stricken beholder, I repeat, here regards God,
who by a just and secret judgment neither
washes away the evil actions of those who are
reprobate nor accepts their good actions; and,
moreover, he hardens their hearts, lest they
should perchance repent and return and be

converted, and he should heal them. Nor is this without a sure and eternal reason, which is manifestly so much the more awful as it is, in fact, immovable and eternal. That is a very fearful saying upon this subject which we read in the prophet, where God speaking to his angels, says: "Let us have pity on the wicked" (Isa. 26:10). And when they are stricken with terror and inquire: "Will he then, not learn to do righteousness?" No, he replies; and he adds the reason: "In the land of righteousness will he deal unjustly, and will not behold the majesty of the Lord. . . ."

Who, then, in seeing that he whose judgments are like the great deep spares and pities such persons in this life, in order not to spare them in eternity, will seek rest in this place? This vision is filled with the tremor of judgment, not with the peace and security of the bedchamber of the King. Terrible is that place, and wholly devoid of calm and rest. When brought into it, I shudder to the very heart, and revolve in my mind with fear that saying: "Who knoweth whether he be worthy of love or of hatred?" (Eccles. 9:1). Nor is it wonderful if I (who am but as a leaf driven to and fro, or as the dry stubble—Job 13:25) should totter in that place, where that great man who contemplated with such marvelous insight (the doings of the Creator), declares that his feet were almost gone and his treadings had well nigh slipt, saying: "I was envious of the foolish, when I saw the prosperity of the wicked." Wherefore? Because "they are not in trouble as other men, neither are they plagued like other men; therefore pride compasseth them about as a chain" (Ps. 73:3-6), that they should not be humbled and made penitent, but be condemned, because of their pride, with the devil, who is proud, and with his angels. For those who have no part in the trouble of men shall assuredly have part in that of demons, and shall hear that terrible sentence from the mouth of the Judge: "Depart from me, ye cursed, into everlasting fire, prepared for the devil and his angels" (Matt. 25:41). And yet this too is a habitation of God; it is plainly no other than the house of God and the gate of heaven. It is here that God is feared; here is his name holy and terrible; it is as it were, the entering in of his glory; for "the fear of the Lord is the beginning of wisdom" (Ps. 111:10).

Let it not astonish you that I have set down the beginning of wisdom as belonging to this, and not to the earlier place. For as we listen to wisdom teaching of all things as a professor in his lecture-hall, so we receive these teachings in ourselves; there we are indeed instructed but here we are touched and influenced. Instruction renders men learned, but feeling makes them wise. The sun does not render all things warm upon which its light falls, so wisdom also instructs many persons what they ought to do, without going on to give the earnestness and ardor needful to do it. It is one thing to know of the existence of great treasures, another to possess them; and it is the possession, not the knowledge, which renders a man rich. Similarly, there is a difference between the knowledge of God and the fear of God, and it is not the knowledge, but the fear of him, which renders a man truly wise, provided it be a fear which makes (a durable) impression on the soul. Would you call a person wise whom his own acquirements render vain? It is only the most foolish of persons who would call those wise, who, when they had known God, glorified him not as God, nor rendered thanks to him. For my part, I am rather of the apostle's opinion, when he says that their heart was manifestly foolish (Rom. 1: 21, 22). And truly "the fear of the Lord is the beginning of wisdom," because the soul begins to have discernment of and inclination for God when he has stricken it with fear, not when he has communicated to it knowledge. If you fear the righteousness of God, if you fear his power, then, inasmuch as he is righteous and powerful, you incline to him with preference and choice; for fear is a kind of preference. It (preference) renders one wise, as knowledge makes one knowing, and riches render one rich. To what purpose, then, is the former place? It serves only to prepare us for wisdom. There you are prepared for it that here you may enter upon its possession. The preparation for it is the attainment of a certain degree of knowledge. But this is followed only too easily by the elation of vanity, unless this be represt by fear; and therefore it is rightly said, ''The fear of the Lord is the beginning of wisdom,'' since this fear first opposes itself to that which the apostle declares is foolishness. The former, then, gives a certain approach, as it were, to wisdom, but the latter an entrance into it. Nevertheless, the beholder finds perfect rest neither in the one nor in the other, because in the one God appears, as it were, full of care, in the other full of trouble. Seek not, then, the bedchamber of the Bridegroom in these spots, whereof the one resembles rather the audience chamber of a professor, the other the tribunal of a judge.

But there is a place where God is beheld as

truly tranquil and in repose; it is in fact, the
place, not of a judge, not of a teacher, but of
a Bridegroom. I do not know how it may
be with regard to others, but as far as con-
cerns myself, that is for me a chamber into
which entrance has sometimes been granted
unto me; but, alas! how rarely that has happened, and for how short a time it has lasted!
It is there that is clearly recognized the mercy
of the Lord from everlasting and to everlasting upon them that fear him. Happy is
he who can say "I am a companion of all
them that fear thee, and of them that keep
thy precepts" (Ps. 119: 63). The decree of
the Lord standeth fast; his purpose of peace
endureth upon them who fear him, forgiving
the evil actions, and rewarding the good which
they have done, and, by a marvelous method
of his mercy, making not only those things
which are good, but also those which are evil,
work together for their good. O truly blest,
and, indeed, the only blest one is he "unto
whom the Lord will not impute iniquity"
(Ps. 32: 2). For there is none without sin,
no not one; for "all have sinned and come
short of the glory of God" (Rom. 3: 23).
But "who shall lay anything to the charge
of God's elect?" (Rom. 8: 33). It is sufficient for all righteousness to me to have him
upon my side against whom alone I have of-

fended. Everything which he has decreed
not to impute unto me is as tho it had not
been. Not to sin is the righteousness of God,
but the forgiveness of God is the righteousness of man. I have seen these things and
can bear witness to the truth of that saying:
"Whosoever is born of God doth not commit
sin, for his seed abideth in him" (1 John
3:9). Now, the heavenly seed is the eternal
predestination, wherewith God hath loved his
elect and bestowed graces upon them in his
Beloved Son before the foundation of the
world; beholding them in him with favor,
that they might be rendered worthy to see
his power and his glory, and be made sharers
in the inheritance of him to whose image and
likeness they were to be conformed. These,
then, I have looked upon as having never
sinned, because, even tho they are seen to
have sinned in time, their offenses do not
appear in eternity, because the charity of
their Father covers the multitude of sins.
He calls them blessed, then, "whose iniquities
are forgiven, and whose sins are covered"
(Ps. 32:1). Then I have felt on a sudden
so great a joy and confidence arising in me
that it surpassed the fear which had gone before it in the place of horror—I mean in that
of the second vision—and it seemed to me as
if I were one of those blessed ones. O that it

had lasted longer! Again and again do thou
visit me O Lord with thy salvation, "that I
may see the good of thy chosen, that I may
rejoice in the gladness of thy nation" (Ps.
106: 4, 5).

O place of true repose, which I may not
unfitly call by the name of chamber! O place
in which God is beheld, not, as it were, aroused
and in wrath nor as distracted with care,
but in which is experienced the influence of
his good and favorable and perfect will!
That vision does not terrify, but soothes; it
does not arouse an unjust curiosity, but al-
lays it, and tranquilizes the spirit in place
of wearying it. Here true rest is felt. The
God of peace renders all things peaceful, and
the soul looking up with fixt gaze at his
ineffable stillness, is itself awed into quiescence. It is as if one beheld some king or
great judge, who, after the hearing of causes
in his court all the day long, dismisses his
crowd of attendants, puts an end to the labors
of his office, returns with night to his peaceful palace, enters into his chamber with those
few companions whom he condescends to
honor with his intimacy in private, and there
enjoys his repose with the more confidence
because it is in such complete retirement,
and because, as he looks peacefully around,
he sees only the faces of those who are dear

to him. If it should ever be the happy lot of any of you to be caught up and withdrawn for awhile into that hidden and mysterious sanctuary of God, and not to be called away from it either by the needs of the body, by the sting of some care, or, it may be, by the haunting pang of some sin, or at least by the inrushing flood of ideas and images belonging to this world, which are very difficult indeed to banish, such an one will be able in truth, when he returns to us again, to lift up his head and say: "The King hath brought me into his chamber." And yet I would not rashly affirm that this would have been that very chamber into which the Bride rejoices to have entered. It is indeed a chamber, and the chamber of the King; but of the three, that we have pointed out as included in the threefold vision, there is that one alone in repose and peace. For, as we have already shown, in the first chamber there is but a brief and fleeting repose, and in the second none whatever; because in the first God is beheld as wonderful and admirable, and the curiosity is violently excited to search out the numerous instances of his glory; while in the second he is beheld as terrible, and human weakness is thrown into terror at the sight of him. But in the third he is beheld not as terrible, and he even deigns to appear not so much admirable as lovable, serene, and peaceful, sweet and gentle, and full of mercy toward them who look unto him.

Now that you may retain in memory a brief summary of what I have said to you about the cellar, the garden and the chamber of the Bridegroom, remember that there are three times, three merits, and three kinds of reward. In the garden take note of the times; in the cellar of the merits; and in the bedchamber of the rewards, in that three-fold contemplation of the soul that is seeking and searching for the chamber of the King.

A Prayer of James Russell Miller

O God, our heavenly Father, we thy children come now to thy feet with our supplications. We can not live without thy blessing. Life is too hard for us, and duty is too large. We get discouraged, and our feeble hands hang down. We come to thee with our weakness asking thee for strength. Help us always to be of good cheer. Let us not be disheartened by difficulties. Let us never doubt thy love or any of thy promises. Give us grace to be encouragers of others, never discouragers. Let us not go about with sadness or fear among men, but may we be a benediction to every one we meet, always making life easier, never harder, for those who come within our influence. Help us to be as Christ to others, that they may see something of his love in our lives and learn to love him in us. We beseech thee to hear us, to receive our prayer, and to forgive our sins, for Jesus Christ's sake. AMEN.

The Canticle of the Sun

BY

SAINT FRANCIS OF ASSISI

FRANCIS OF ASSISI

(GIOVANNI BERNARDONE)

Founder of the Franciscan order; born in
Assisi, Central Italy, in 1182, and died there
October 3, 1226. His father, a merchant, gave the
boy a good education. In 1201 he joined a mili-
tary expedition against Perugia, was taken
prisoner, and spent a year as a captive. It is
said "that when he began to avoid the sports of
his former companions, and they asked him laugh-
ingly if he were thinking of marrying," he
answered, "Yes, a fairer bride than any you have
ever seen"—meaning his "Lady Poverty," as
he afterward used to say. He spent much time
in lonely places, asking God for enlightenment.
"By degrees he took to nursing the most repulsive
victims in the lazar-houses near Assisi. After a
pilgrimage to Rome, he had a vision in which he
heard a voice calling upon him to restore the
Church of God which had fallen into decay." In
the year 1209, as the result of a sermon on Matthew
10:9, he decided to devote himself wholly to a
life of poverty. Later on he was joined by eleven
other companions, who devoted themselves to service in the "abodes of sickness and poverty."
The canticle known as *Laudes creaturarum*, with
its childlike invocations to "Brother Sun, Sister
Moon with the stars, Brother Wind, Sister Water,
Brother Fire, and finally Sister Death, to raise
their voices to the glory of God," dates from
about 1221. His works consist of sermons, treatises, letters, proverbs, and hymns.

Francis of Assisi

(In the holy cave at Sublaco)

The Canticle

Almighty, most high, good Lord God, thine are the glory, praise, honor, and all blessing! To thee alone, Almighty, do they belong and no man is worthy to speak thy name. Praise be to thee, O Lord, for all thy creatures and especially for our brother the sun who gives us the day and who shows forth thy light. Fair is he and radiant with great splendor. To us he is the symbol of thee, O Lord. Praise be to thee, O Lord, for our sister the moon and for the stars. Thou hast set them clear, beautiful and precious in the heaven above. Praise be to thee, O Lord, for our brother the wind, for the air and the clouds, for the clear sky and for all weathers by which thou givest life and the means of life to all thy creatures. Praise be to thee, O Lord, for our sister water who is so serviceable to us, humble also, precious and chaste. Praise be to thee, O Lord, for our brother fire, by whom thou givest us light in the darkness; he is beautiful and bright, courageous and strong. Praise be to thee, O Lord, for our mother the earth, who sustains us and nourishes us, bringing forth divers fruits, flowers of many colors and the

By kind permission of Messrs. Duffield & Co.

grass. Praise be to thee, O Lord, for all those who are forgiving one to another for his love's sake and who endure weakness and tribulation; blessed are they who shall endure peaceably, for thou, O Most Highest, shall give them a crown. Praise be to thee, O Lord, for our sister the death of the body whom no man can escape. Wo unto him that dieth in mortal sin. Blessed are they who are found walking according to thy most holy will for the second death shall be powerless to do them harm. Praise ye and bless ye the Lord and give thanks unto him and serve him with great humility.

An Ancient Collect

Almighty Lord our God, direct our steps into the way of peace, and strengthen our hearts to obey thy commands; may the day-spring visit us from on high, and give light to those who sit in darkness and the shadow of death; that they may adore thee for thy mercy, follow thee for thy truth, desire thee for thy sweetness, who art the blessed Lord God of Israel. AMEN.

SELECTIONS FROM

The Works of
Jan van Ruysbroeck

From the Translation

by

EARLE BAILLIE

JAN VAN RUYSBROECK

Dutch (Flemish) mystic; born at Ruysbroeck, 1294; died at the Augustinian monastery of Groenendael, December 2, 1381. At the home of his uncle, canon of St. Gudula, he studied diligently for four years and then determined to renounce secular learning for theology. At the age of twenty-four he became a priest and vicar of St. Gudula's; and in 1343 retired to the Groenendael monastery, where he spent the rest of his life as prior. Soon after his death, legend gathered around his name, and at an early date he was styled *Doctor ecstaticus*. His works were translated into Latin by his pupils, and translations into High German and into the dialects of Gelderland, Cologne, and the Upper Rhine are extant.

The Effects of Love—Humility and Thanksgiving

What is love in itself? No one knows anything about it, but some of its effects are known.

The eternal love sheds abroad light and grace in all the powers of the soul; hence are the virtues. The grace of God touches and moves the higher forces; thence flow charity, light, love of justice, adoration of the divine plan discerning and active; thence, fidelity superior to images, victory without fatigue, and that sublime inanition, at the same time active and fruitful, by which a man rises above himself into the unity of the Spirit. Love gives more than we are able to receive and exacts more than we are able to give. Its requirements are like a devouring fire: the body shares the impatience of the soul; the spirit burns with a consuming eagerness. This panting avidity recollects the spirit in the simple peace of the deep.

The Spirit comes in contact with our spirit and says to it in the depth: "Love me as I love thee, as I have loved thee eternally." Now this voice, this prayer, this interior demand, is so terrible to hear that our spirit is utterly overthrown by the tempest of love; and all the powers of the soul, shaken and trembling, turn to each other asking, "do we indeed love the eternal Love, the Love inexhaustible?"

When a man considers in the depth of his heart the immensity of God and his faithfulness; when he reflects on his essence, his love, his benefits, which add nothing to his beatitude, and looking on himself proceeds to count up his offenses against this infinite and faithful Lord, he turns against himself with such indignation and contempt that he knows not how to give expression to it or to despise himself sufficiently.

He feels that the contempt which he deserves is greater than that which he is able to conceive. The best thing which he can do in this difficulty is to complain to God, his Lord and his Friend, of the weakness of his self-contempt, unable to place him as low as he desires.

Sin is so terrible an evil that, neither to attain any conceivable good nor to avoid any possible ill, is it allowable to commit one single sin mortal or venial. But we have committed many. How is it that we can contain ourselves? that we do not melt and fail with adoring love when we plunge into this abyss of mercy, the eyes of our soul being open to the truth that God has taken away our sins?

He has restored friendship with his enemies; how is it that we do not melt away?

Truly, the creation of the world, drawn from nothingness, is a small thing compared with pardon! But this is not all; the Lord, in his clemency, has willed to turn our sins against themselves and in our favor. He has found the means of making them of service to us, and of converting them into instruments of salvation in our hands. Let not this truth diminish our fear of sin, or our grief at having been guilty of it; but sin has brought us to penance, it has become for us a source of humility and love.

It is important, however, to observe that there is a source of humility much higher than this. The Blessed Virgin Mary, conceived without sin, possest a more sublime humility than Mary Magdalene. The latter was pardoned, the former was guiltless; and this absolute immunity, grander than all pardon, caused a higher thanksgiving to ascend from earth to heaven than did the conversion of Magdalene.

Humility, says Gilbert, has such a tendency toward the depths that it can not rest till it has got to the bottom, which is the abode of joy. The bottom of the abyss is the absence of all spirit of inordinate appropriation; but so long as we are in this world we have always something of which to dispossess ourselves, some garment to lay aside. Humility, like charity, is always capable of increase; we must therefore ever seek to reach a lower depth.

To be plunged in humility is, it seems to me, to be plunged in God; for God is below the abyss, above all and beneath all. When we are so profoundly lost in God that giving to him or receiving from him becomes one and the same thing to us, then we begin to be content with our impotence.

Since a fundamental humility is the pure and solid vessel capable of receiving grace, and into which alone God wills to pour it forth, I earnestly conjure you to be humble. Humility is so precious that it obtains things too great to be exprest. Every ascent has humility for its condition and laws. He who possesses a good foundation of humility does not need many words for his instruction; God teaches him more than he can make known to others. Such men are the disciples of God.

Humility gives birth to liberty and confidence. The liberty which grows along with humility exalts man's powers into thanksgiving; but if the humble man had a power of praise greater than that of all creatures put together, it would still be insufficient in his eyes. He could never place God high enough

or himself low enough; but here is a marvel;
—this impotence turns into wisdom, and the
very insufficiency of his act becomes the chief
happiness of his life. . . .

We must not forget that thanksgiving is
the first act of the creature, and that this act
will endure as long as eternity. When
Michael and his angels fought against Lucifer
and his angels, the latter were cast down
like lightning (for "he that exalteth himself
shall be abased"); while the former began
the eternal act of thanksgiving, and all the
choirs of angels who remained faithful in-
toned the hymn which will never end, praising
God for their victory, because he is their God
and his love as eternal as his glory and their
joy.

The Three Books

Ever ere thou goest to thy nightly couch
place before thee three books which thou
must continually possess. The first is old,
worm-eaten, musty, written in the blackest
of characters; the second is white and beautiful, with red writing; the third glitters in
golden letters. First, thou shalt read the
old book; that is to say, contemplate thy past
life, which, in common with all mortals, is
black in guilt and sorrow. Go in and open

the door of conscience, which at the last
judgment of Christ shall be displayed before
God and the universe. Reflect on the evil of
thy ways, how indifferent thou hast been in
words, works, wishes, and thoughts; cast down
thine eyes with the publican and say, "God
be merciful to me, a sinner. O Lord I have
sinned, I have sinned, do thou have mercy
upon me!" Then shall the Lord drive from
thee fear and anguish, and bestow upon thee
faith and hope. He will excite within thee
the desire to praise him, and will make thee
faithful even unto death. Now lay aside
the old book, and fetch from thy memory the
white one. Behold, this is the spotless life of
Christ, typical of his pure soul, and written
in red, in remembrance of his crown of thorns
and bleeding wounds. These are the red letters which witness to us his undying love.
Gaze upon them in sympathy, and bless him
that he has opened to thee the gates of heaven,
and prepared for thee a place therein. Lastly,
raise thine eyes to the heights, and read there
the golden writing of the third book; that is,
contemplate the glories of eternal life, compared to which all earthly brightness disap-
pears, as torchlight in the blaze of the mid-
day sun.

SELECTIONS FROM

The Little Book of Eternal Wisdom

AND

The Maxims

BY

HEINRICH SUSO

HEINRICH SUSO (AMANDUS VON BERG)

German mystic, born at Ueberlingen, near Constance, March 31, 1300; died at Ulm, Jan. 25, 1366. Out of devotion to his mother, who was a person of eminent holiness, he called himself by her maiden name of Seuss, Latinized into Suso, instead of taking his father's surname Von Berg. He entered the Dominican monastery when only thirteen years of age. While studying in Strasburg and Cologne, in his twenty-eighth year, he came under the influence and teaching of Eckhart, whom he defended from the charge of heresy. Suso "practised asceticism until his fortieth year, when his system was so exhausted that in order to save his body he was forced to discontinue it." In his dispute with Louis of Bavaria, he sided with the pope, and was banished from Constance and sent to Diessenhoven (1339-1346). Here he began to work as an itinerant preacher. He subsequently retired to Ulm, passing his later years in the Dominican monastery there. Among Suso's writings are the following: the so-called "Exemplar," a collection of four treatises with a prolog: (1) the "Biography"; (2) "Little Book of Eternal Wisdom"; (3) "Little Book of Truth"; (4) "Little Book of Letters," to which was added an unabridged book of letters. A fifth work is "Horologium Sapientiae"; a sixth consisted of "Sermons," and there was possibly a seventh, the "Minnebüchlein."

Little Book of Eternal Wisdom

How Lovely God Is

The Servitor.[1]—Lord, let me reflect on that divine passage, where thou speakest of thyself in the Book of Wisdom: "Come over to me, all ye that desire me, and be filled with my fruits. I am the mother of fair love; my spirit is sweet above honey and the honeycomb. Wine and music rejoice the heart, but the love of wisdom is above them both" (Ecclus. 24:24, 26, 27; 40:20).

Ah, Lord! Thou canst show thyself so lovely and so tender, that all hearts must needs languish for thee and endure, for thy sake, all the misery of tender desire; thy words of love flow so sweetly out of thy sweet mouth, and so powerfully affect many hearts in their blooming days, that perishable love is wholly extinguished in them. O my dear Lord, this it is for which my soul sighs, this it is which makes my spirit sad, this it is about which I would gladly hear thee speak. Now, then, my only elected Comforter, speak one little word to my soul, to thy poor hand-

[1] This work is cast throughout in the form of a dialog. The author calls himself "The Servitor."

maid; for, lo! I am fallen softly asleep beneath thy shadow, and my heart watcheth.

Eternal Wisdom.—Listen, then, my son, and see, incline to me thy ears, enter wholly into thy interior, and forget thyself and all things. I am in myself the incomprehensible good, which always was and always is, which never was and never will be uttered. I may, indeed, give myself to men's hearts to be felt by them, but no tongue can truly express me in words. And yet, when I, the supernatural, immutable good, present myself to every creature according to its capacity to be susceptible of me, I bind the sun's splendor, as it were, in a cloth, and give thee spiritual perception of me and my sweet love in bodily words thus: I set myself tenderly before the eyes of thy heart; now adorn and clothe thou me in spiritual perceptions and represent me as delicate and as comely as thy very heart could wish, and bestow on me all those things that can move the heart to especial love and entire delight of soul. Lo! all and everything that thou and all men can possibly imagine of form, of elegance, and grace, is in me far more ravishing than any one can express, and in words like these do I choose to make myself known. Now, listen further: I am of high birth, of noble race; I am the Eternal Word of the fatherly heart, in which, ac-

cording to the love-abounding abyss of my
natural sonship in his sole paternity, I possess a gratefulness before his tender eyes in
the sweet and bright-flaming love of the
Holy Ghost. I am the throne of delight, I
am the crown of salvation, my eyes are so
clear, my mouth so tender, my cheeks so radiant and blooming, and all my figure so fair
and ravishing, yea, and so delicately formed,
that if a man were to lie in a glowing furnace
till the day of judgment, only to have one
single glance at my beauty, he would not deserve it. See, I am so deliciously adorned
in garments of light, I am so exquisitely set
off with all the blooming colors of living
flowers, that all May-blossoms, all the beautiful shrubs of all dewy fields, all the tender
buds of the sunny meads, are but as rough
thistles compared to my adornment.

> In the Godhead I play the game of bliss,
> Such joy the angels find in this,
> That unto them a thousand years
> But as one little hour appears.

All the heavenly host follow me entranced
by new wonders, and behold me; their eyes
are fixt on mine; their hearts are inclined to
me, their minds bent on me without inter-
mission. Happy is he who, in joyous security, shall take me by my beautiful hand,

and join in my sweet diversions, and dance
for ever the dance of joy amid the ravishing
delights of the kingdom of heaven! One little
word there spoken by my sweet mouth will
far surpass the singing of all the angels, the
music of all harps, the harmony of all sweet
strings. My faithfulness is so made to be
loved, so lovely am I to be embraced, and so
tender for pure languishing souls to kiss, that
all hearts ought to break for my possession.
I am condescending and full of sympathy and
always present to the pure soul. I abide
with her in secret, at table, in bed, in the
streets, in the fields. Turn myself whichever
way I will, in me there is nothing that can
displease, in me is everything that can delight
the utmost wishes of thy heart and desires of
the soul. Lo! I am a good so pure, that he
who in his day only gets one drop of me regards all the pleasures and delights of this
world as nothing but bitterness; and its possessions and honors as worthless, and only fit
to be cast away; my beloved ones are encom-
passed by my love, and are absorbed into the
one thing alone without imaged love and
without spoken words, and are taken and in-
fused into that good out of which they flowed.
My love can also relieve regenerate hearts
from the heavy load of sin, and can give a
free, pure, and gentle heart, and create a

clean conscience. Tell me, what is there in all this world able to outweigh this one thing? For he who gives his heart wholly to me lives joyfully, dies securely, and obtains the kingdom of heaven here as well as hereafter.

An Explanation of How God Can Appear So Wrathful and Yet Be So Gracious

The Servitor.—Three things there are at which I marvel very much; one is, that thou shouldst be beyond all measure so amiable thyself, and yet so severe a judge of evil deeds, Lord, when I reflect on thy severe justice, my heart with passionate voice exclaims: "Woe to all who persist in sin!" for did they but know the strict account of every single sin, which thou wilt infallibly require, even from thy very dearest friends, they ought sooner to pluck out their teeth and hair than ever provoke thy anger! Wo is me! How very terrible is thy angry countenance, how very intolerable thy ungentle averted looks! So full of fire are thy threatening words that they cut through heart and soul. Shield me, O Lord, from thy wrathful countenance, and extend not thy vengeance against me to the next world. Lo! when I only doubt lest, because of my guilty deeds, thou mayest have turned thy face angrily away from me, it is a thing so insupportable that nothing in all this world is so bitter to me. Oh, my Lord and Father, how could my heart endure thy angry countenance for ever! When I but seriously reflect on thy countenance inflamed with anger, my soul is so horrified, all my strength is so shaken, that I can liken it to nothing else but the heavens beginning to darken and grow black, to fire raging in the clouds, and a mighty thunder rending them, so that the earth trembles, and fiery bolts dart down upon men. Lord, let no one confide in thy silence, for verily thy silence will soon be turned to dreadful thunder. Lord, the angry countenance of thy fatherly anger, to that man who is fearful of provoking and losing thee, is a hell above all hells. I will say nothing of that furious countenance of thine which the wicked at the last day will have to behold in bitterness of heart. Wo, everlasting wo to those who shall have to expect so great a calamity!

Lord, all this is a profound mystery to my heart, and yet thou sayest that thou art so gracious and so good.

Eternal Wisdom.—I am the immutable good, and subsist the same and am the same. But that I do not appear the same, arises from the difference of those who view me differently, according as they are with or without sin. I am tender and loving in my nature, and yet a terrible judge of evil deeds. I require from my friends childlike awe and confiding love, in order that awe may restrain them from sin and love unite them to me in faith.

A Prayer To Be Said When Thou Goest To Receive Our Lord's Holy Body

O thou living fruit, thou sweet blossom, thou delicious paradise apple of the blooming fatherly heart, thou sweet vine of Cyprus in the vineyard of Engedi, who will give me to receive thee so worthily this day that thou shalt desire to come to me, to dwell with me, and never to separate from me! O unfathomable Good, that fillest heaven and earth, incline thyself graciously this day, and despise not thy poor creature. Lord, if I am not worthy of thee, yet do I stand in need of thee. Ah, gentle Lord, art thou not he who with one word created heaven and earth? Lord, with one word canst thou restore health to my sick soul. O Lord, do unto me accordingly to thy grace, according to thy infinite mercy, and not according to my deserts. Yes, thou art the innocent Paschal Lamb, which at this day is still offered up for the sins of all mankind. Ah, thou sweet-tasting Bread of Heaven, which contains all sweet tastes according to the desire of every one's heart, make the hungry mouth of my soul to rejoice in thee this day; give me to eat and to drink; strengthen, adorn, and unite me interiorly to thee. Ah, Eternal Wisdom, come down so powerfully this day into my soul, that all my enemies may be driven out of her, all my crimes be melted away, and all my sins be forgiven. Enlighten my understanding with the light of true faith. Inflame my will with thy sweet love. Cheer up my mind with thy glad presence, and give virtue and perfection to all my powers. Watch over me at my death, that I may enjoy thy beatific vision in eternal bliss. AMEN.

Maxims

Maxims, Conformable To Right Reason, For the Guidance of An Exterior Man Into His Interior

Let thy walk be an interior one, and be not given to break out either in words or in thy walk.

Act according to the truth in simplicity, and, whatever happens, be not helpful to thyself; for he who helps himself too much will not be helped by the truth.

When thou art with men pay no heed to what thou seest or hearest, and cleave to that alone which has shown itself to thee (*i.e.*, remember God alone who has shown himself to thee under these outward things).

Be careful that in thy actions thy reason goes first; for when the sensual appetite gets the start, every evil comes of it.

God wishes not to deprive us of pleasure; but he wishes to give us pleasure in its totality; that is to say, all pleasure.

The more mightily thou humblest thyself, the higher thou shalt be exalted.

He who wishes to dwell in his inmost interior must rid himself of all multiplicity. We must habitually reject all that is not the one thing.

Where the sensual appetite is the moving principle of a man's actions, there is toil, suffering, and mental darkness.

What greater pleasure is there than to find myself the one thing that I ought to be, and the whole thing that I ought to be? (*i.e.*, one with God, who is one and all.)

A man should remain stedfast in his state of freedom from mental images, and of self-restraint. Herein lies the greatest delight.

In what does a truly detached man exercise himself? In annihilating himself.

When a man detaches himself from himself without allowing the sensual appetite to break out, he destroys self. If he acted otherwise, he would be helping himself by means of his sensual appetite.

When our love is given to a sensible image or person, it is accident, loving accident, and this we have no right to do; nevertheless I bear with myself in this until I get quit of it. It is, however, an interiorly simple act, when a man does not love the image which is present to him, but when all things are to him one, and that one is God.

Keep thy feelings within thee both in weal and wo; for a man who does this loves more in one year than one who lets his feelings break out, loves in three.

Some men are to be met with who have had an interior drawing from God, and have not followed it. The interior and exterior of these men are far apart, and it is in this that many fail.

Take heed not to break out exteriorly in a way unlike the (divine and interior) pattern.

A man should be on his guard against the inclination which leads him to catch at everything which may save him from having to yield to the invitations of the simple truth. If thou wilt not submit to be simple, thou wilt have to submit to be manifold.

Wilt thou be of use to all creatures, turn thyself away from all creatures.

Live as if there were no creature on earth but thee.

Nature loves nature and makes itself its aim. Some men's nature has not been sufficiently crusht, and when this happens, they continue exterior.

The power of refraining from things gives a man more power than would the possession of the things.

One deflection from the right course brings along with it another.

See that nature in thee is unburdened, and that thy outward man is conformable to thy inward man.

Look well to the inward man; for on this depends thy exterior and interior life.

It belongs to perfect detachment to keep nature at all times bridled.

A man should never lose sight of himself, lest nature should run away.

Thou lamentest that thou art still too active, undetached, and impatient. Nevertheless, despair not. The more keenly thou feelest this, the better.

Perishable love is a root of all vices, and a cloak of all truth.

The setting of the sensual nature is the rising of the truth. When the powers of the soul have ceased to work, and the elements have been purified, the powers remain fixt upon their eternal object, if they have been directed toward it according to their ability.

To be worsted is to gain the victory in the estimation of God's friends (Matt. 5:39).

There is nothing pleasurable save what is uniform with the most inmost depths of the divine nature.

Our nature in its present state is richly endowed. The more it goes out of itself, the further it is from God; and the more it turns inward the nearer to him it is.

He who has attained to the purification of the senses in God performs so much the better all the operations of the senses.

If a man subjects his nature, when it has been purified, to the truth, his nature is guided in such sort that it performs much more perfectly all exterior actions. Otherwise it wastes itself upon temporal matters, and can do nothing really well.

Purity, intelligence, and virtue give a feeling of wealth to those who possess them. When the sensible possession of these virtues is withdrawn from such persons by God, it sometimes happens that they die to all creatures. Those who profit by this withdrawal are brought nigher to God by it.

What is that which drives a man to pursue evil courses? It is the craving for something which may satisfy him. Yet we can only find this in abnegation, and not in evil courses.

The reason why some men so often fall into a faulty sadness is that they do not at all times keep an eye upon themselves to avoid in everything doing what deserves punishment.

If a man can not comprehend the matter, let him be passive; and the matter will comprehend him.

Abide within thyself. The plea of seeking things outside thee presents itself as a necessity; but it is only a way of helping self.

Remain stedfastly in thyself until thou art drawn out of thyself without any act of thine.

We should not move until we have observed whether it be God or nature that is working in us.

Take care that nature works in thee its works from out itself without the concurrence of other causes.

A truly detached man should attend to four things. First, he should be very virtuous in his walk, that things may flow from him without him. Secondly, he should also be virtuous and quiet with regard to his senses, and not carry tales hither and thither, for this is calculated to fill his mind with images. Thus his interior senses will be able to act inactively. Thirdly, he should not be given to attach himself; and he should take care that there is nothing heterogeneous in him. Fourthly, he should not be contentious, but he should behave lovingly to those by whom God may be pleased to purify him.

All the powers have one object and one work, and this is to be conformed to the eternal truth.

It is bad to begin many things and to bring none to an end.

Observe whether the intimacy between good people arises from inclination or from simplicity. The first is far too common.

Offer not thyself too much to anyone. Those please least who offer most.

An interior humble walk beseems thee. When a thing acts in opposition to its nature, it is always unbecoming to it.

Happy the man whose words and ways are few. The more words and ways there are in any man, the more there is of what is accidental. Stay within thyself, and be not like such men, otherwise thou wilt suffer for it.

Some men act from their sensible feelings both in suffering and in joy; but a man should not look to himself in this.

Our eyes should not look outward, except to rid ourselves of interior images.

In the spiritual annihilation of self the final consummation is attained. When Christ had said "Into thy hands I commend my spirit," he added immediately, "It is consummated."

God and the devil are in man. He who guides himself and he who forsakes himself discover the difference (*i.e.*, the self-willed find in themselves hell, and the detached heaven).

He who desires to have rest at all times must be on his guard against himself in this as in everything else (*i.e.*, this desire is a species of self-seeking).

He who is interior amid exterior things is much more interior than he who is only interior when within himself.

It is good for a man to guide himself in nothing; and he is on the right road who contemplates under the forms of things their eternal essences.

A detached man is always interiorly alike.

When a man still complains and is impatient, all this springs from imperfection. It must therefore be got rid of.

There are many more reasoning men than simple men. Those are called reasoning men in whom reason rules. But the simple man, through his inaction, is freed from the multiplicity of images which are generated by sensible objects, and he does not contemplate things as sensible, for simplicity has become his nature, and he is like a vessel (full of God) and like a child.

How happy is the man who abides stedfast against multiplicity. What a sensible entrance he has into familiar intercourse with heaven.

A good intention often impedes true union.

We should bear as regularly with that part of us which comes from Adam (*i.e.*, the consequences of the fall) as with that by which we attain eternal bliss.

He who wishes to possess all things must become as nothing to himself and all things.

Wouldst thou be a detached man? Take care that, however God may act toward thee, whether directly by himself or indirectly by his creatures, thou abidest always the same, by a complete renunciation of what is thine.

All those who allow themselves a wrong liberty make themselves their own aim and object.

A detached man must be unformed from the forms and images of creatures; he must be formed upon Christ and transformed into the Godhead.

He who regards himself in Christ lets all things follow their rightful course.

When a man has died to self and begun to live in Christ, it is well with him.

When a man strives by turning inward to conform himself to the truth, it is clearly brought home to him that he had gone forth out of himself, and he observes that there is still something of the creature in him, on which the attraction acted. In this he bears with himself, and perceives that he has not yet ceased from all action. Now, thus to bear with self is to become simple. The going out of self produces a kind of weariness; but when he has turned away from creatures this weariness passes off.

What is a truly detached man's object in all things? It is to die to himself; and when he dies to himself all things die to him.

What is the least obstacle? It is a thought. What is the greatest obstacle? It is when the soul abides in the obstinacy of its self-will.

A detached man should not let any moment pass away unmarked.

A detached man should not be always looking to see what he needs, but he should be always looking to see what he can do without.

If a detached man wishes to conform himself to the truth, he must in the first place be diligent in turning inward from things of sense, for God is a spirit. Secondly, he must take note whether he has attached himself to any obstacle (*i.e.*, anything which stands between him and God). Thirdly, he must observe whether he is his own guide in anything, owing to the sensual appetite having got the start. Fourthly, he must, in the light which fills his soul, consider the presence of the all-penetrating divine essence in him, and that he is one of its vessels.

The more a man turns away from himself and all created things, the more perfect are the union and bliss to which he attains.

Rest on nothing which is not God.

Keep thy senses closed to every image which may present itself. Be empty of everything which the outward-gazing mind selects, which takes captive the will and brings earthly joy or delight into the heart.

If thou art where a sin or imperfection is committed, add not aught of thine to it, and have nothing to do with it.

He who always dwells with himself becomes possest of very ample means.

The recreation which a detached man grants to his nature should be confined to strict necessity, and it should be taken in harmless occupations, from which he can readily and without attachment turn away to God.

Gather together and draw in thy soul from the external senses, through which it has dissipated itself upon the multiplicity of outward things.

Be stedfast, and never rest content until thou hast obtained the now of eternity as thy present possession in this life, so far as this is possible to human infirmity.

213

It happened once to a half-detached man, that, on a certain occasion when he had been too self-conscious in suffering, it was said to him: Thou shouldst be so attentive to me and so forgetful of thyself that when thou knowest it is well with me thou shouldst care nothing how it fares with thee.

In the case of a detached man who draws his senses inward from external objects and establishes himself in the inner castle of his soul, the less he finds within to cling to, the more painful are his interior sufferings; and the more quickly he dies, the more swiftly he bursts through to God.

To give the senses a wide field withdraw the man from his interior.

See that thou undertakest nothing which will carry thee out of thyself.

If things come in search of thee, let them not find thee.

Be quick in turning inward into thyself.

A detached man should keep the powers of his soul under such restraint that, on looking within, this is apparent to him.

The more or less detachment a man has, the more or less will he be disturbed by transitory things.

Go in again, and return over and over again into unity, and enjoy God.

Establish thyself in absolute detachment; for an unbounded longing, even for what is divine when it is excessive, may become a secret obstacle.

A detached man remains always inactive as regards himself, just as if he were unconscious of himself; for in that object, which is God, all things are well and harmoniously ordered in him.

Give heed also to thy outward man that it be at one with thy inward man, by the subjection of all fleshly appetites.

To return again into God by detachment is often more pleasing to him than a self-satisfied stability.

Some persons find no hindrance in going out of themselves, but they want stedfastness in this state.

Natural life shows itself in movement and in the operations of the senses. He who detaches himself from himself in this, and dies to himself in stillness, begins a supernatural life.

A Prayer of Thomas Treadwell Stone

We confess unto thee, O God, how weak we are in ourselves, how powerless to do the work of life, how prone to selfishness and sin. We beseech thee to grant us strength, the strength of thy Spirit, the power of thy Christ, wherein we can do all things. Enable us thus to repress every selfish propensity, every wilful purpose, every unkind feeling, every thought and word and deed of anger and impatience, and to cherish perfect love, constant kindness, to think pure thoughts, to speak gentle words, to do helpful and generous deeds. Raise our minds to the contemplation of thy beloved son, that, seeing his divine beauty, we may be drawn near unto him, and changed into his image, and empowered to bring every thought into obedience to Christ, into harmony with his spirit and his immortal life. AMEN.